A passion for CHOCOLATE

MEREDITH ® BOOKS ✳ DES MOINES, IOWA

MEREDITH® PRESS ✳ AN IMPRINT OF MEREDITH® BOOKS

A passion for CHOCOLATE

Editor: Kristi M. Fuller
Senior Associate Art Director: Richard Michels
Photographer: Judd Pilossof, Scott Little *page 35*,
    Mike Dieter *pages 28, 40, 62*
Food Stylists: Liz Duffy, Dianna Nolin *page 35*
Prop Stylist: Lara Hart
Contributing Editor: Linda Henry
Contributing Writer: Marge Perry
Copy Chief: Catherine Hamrick
Copy and Production Editor: Terri Fredrickson
Managers, Book Production: Pam Kvitne, Marjorie J. Schenkelberg
Contributing Copy Editor: Angela Renkoski
Proofreaders: Gretchen Kauffman, Susie Kling, M. Peg Smith
Indexer: Martha Fifield
Electronic Production Coordinator: Paula Forest
Assistants: Judy Bailey, Mary Lee Gavin, Karen Schirm
Test Kitchen Director: Lynn Blanchard
Test Kitchen Product Supervisor: Marilyn Cornelius

MEREDITH® BOOKS
Editor in Chief: James D. Blume
Design Director: Matt Strelecki
Managing Editor: Gregory H. Kayko
Executive Food Editor: Jennifer Dorland Darling

Director, Retail Sales and Marketing: Terry Unsworth
Director, Sales, Special Markets: Rita McMullen
Director, Sales, Premiums: Michael A. Peterson
Director, Sales, Retail: Tom Wierzbicki
Director, Sales, Home & Garden Centers: Ray Wolf
Director, Book Marketing: Brad Elmitt
Director, Operations: George A. Susral
Director, Production: Douglas M. Johnston

Vice President, General Manager: Jamie L. Martin

BETTER HOMES AND GARDENS® MAGAZINE
Editor in Chief: Jean LemMon
Executive Food Editor: Nancy Byal

MEREDITH PUBLISHING GROUP
President, Publishing Group: Christopher M. Little
Vice President, Finance & Administration: Max Runciman

MEREDITH CORPORATION
Chairman and Chief Executive Officer: William T. Kerr

Chairman of the Executive Committee: E. T. Meredith III

All of us at Better Homes and Gardens® Books are dedicated to providing you with the information and ideas you need to create delicious foods. We welcome your comments and suggestions. Write to us at: Better Homes and Gardens Books, Cookbook Editorial Department, 1716 Locust St., Des Moines, IA 50309-3023.

If you would like to purchase any of our books, check wherever quality books are sold. Visit our website at bhg.com or bhgbooks.com

Our seal assures you that every recipe in *A Passion for Chocolate* has been tested in the Better Homes and Gardens® Test Kitchen. This means that each recipe is practical and reliable, and meets our high standards of taste appeal. We guarantee your satisfaction with this book for as long as you own it.

Nostalgic photographs:
H. Armstrong Roberts (pages 45, 66, 79, 93); The Kobal Collection (pages 27, 39, 51, 59); Corbis/Bettman Archive (pages 8, 17); and Archive Photos (page 33).

COOKIES
and
CANDIES

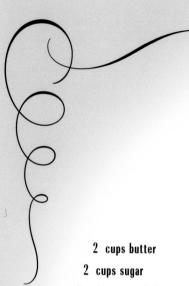

Nut Rocha

2 cups butter

2 cups sugar

2 tablespoons light-color corn syrup

$^1/_3$ cup water

1 11$^1/_2$-ounce package (1$^3/_4$ cups) milk chocolate pieces

1 cup finely chopped toasted nuts (such as almonds, pecans, walnuts, and/or cashews)

MAKES ABOUT 40 SERVINGS

✳ Line a 15×10×1-inch baking pan with foil, extending foil over edges of pan; set aside.

✳ In a 3-quart saucepan melt butter. Stir in sugar, corn syrup, and water. Cook over medium-high heat to boiling, stirring until sugar is dissolved. Avoid splashing sides of pan. Carefully clip a candy thermometer to pan. Cook over medium heat, stirring frequently, until thermometer registers 290°, soft-crack stage (about 15 minutes). Mixture should boil at a moderate, steady rate over entire surface. Remove from heat; remove thermometer.

✳ Pour mixture into prepared pan; spread evenly. Cool about 5 minutes or until top is set. Sprinkle with chocolate pieces; let stand 2 minutes. Spread chocolate over candy. Sprinkle with nuts; press into chocolate. Cool several hours or until set.

✳ Use foil to lift candy out of pan; break into pieces. Store tightly covered.

Crunchy brittle coated with silken chocolate is the ultimate proof that opposites not only attract, but also commingle in harmony.

"YOUR WORDS ARE MY FOOD, YOUR BREATH MY WINE. YOU ARE EVERYTHING TO ME."

–Sarah Bernhardt

Champagne Truffles

PREP TIME: 1½ HOURS   CHILL TIME: 3 HOURS

✳ In a heavy medium saucepan combine semisweet chocolate, butter, and whipping cream. Cook and stir constantly over low heat until chocolate is melted. Gradually stir about half of the hot mixture into the egg yolk. Return entire mixture to the saucepan. Cook and stir over medium heat for 2 minutes. Remove from heat. Stir in champagne or whipping cream. Transfer truffle mixture to a small bowl. Cover and chill about 1 hour or until completely cool and smooth, stirring occasionally.

✳ Beat cooled truffle mixture with an electric mixer on medium speed about 1 minute or until color lightens and mixture is slightly fluffy. Chill about 30 minutes or until mixture holds its shape. Line a baking sheet with waxed paper. Scrape a small ice cream scoop, melon baller, or spoon across the surface of the cold truffle mixture, forming 1-inch balls. Place balls on prepared baking sheet. Cover and chill until firm.

✳ Roll truffles in cocoa powder or powdered sugar. If desired, lightly brush truffles with edible luster dust.

✳ Store truffles in a tightly covered container in the refrigerator for up to 2 weeks.

NOTE: Champagne Truffels shown in photo, page 13.

6   ounces semisweet chocolate, coarsely chopped

¼   cup butter, cut into small pieces

3   tablespoons whipping cream

1   beaten egg yolk

3   tablespoons champagne or whipping cream

Unsweetened cocoa powder or sifted powdered sugar

Edible luster dust (optional)

MAKES 25 TRUFFLES

The seductive luster of champagne combined with the hedonistic pleasure of rich truffles will leave you breathless.

Triple Nut Mocha Fudge

PREP/COOK TIME: 1 HOUR   COOL TIME: 55 MINUTES

2 cups sugar

¾ cup milk

2 ounces unsweetened chocolate, cut up

1 teaspoon instant coffee crystals

1 teaspoon light-colored corn syrup

2 tablespoons butter

2 teaspoons vanilla

⅓ cup chopped walnuts

⅓ cup chopped hazelnuts (filberts)

⅓ cup chopped pecans

MAKES 64 PIECES FUDGE

✳ Line an 8×8×2-inch baking pan with foil, extending foil over edges of pan. Butter foil; set aside.

✳ Butter the sides of a heavy 2-quart saucepan. In saucepan stir together sugar, milk, chocolate, coffee crystals, and corn syrup. Cook over medium-high heat to boiling, stirring constantly with a wooden spoon to dissolve sugar. Avoid splashing mixture on sides of pan.

✳ Carefully clip a candy thermometer to the side of the pan. Cook over medium-low heat, stirring frequently, until thermometer registers 234°, soft-ball stage (20 to 25 minutes). The mixture should boil at a moderate, steady rate over the entire surface.

✳ Remove saucepan from the heat. Add butter and vanilla, but do not stir. Cool, without stirring, to 110° (about 55 minutes).

✳ Remove candy thermometer from saucepan. Beat mixture vigorously with a wooden spoon until fudge begins to thicken. Add nuts. Continue beating until fudge becomes very thick and starts to lose its gloss (about 10 minutes).

✳ Immediately spread fudge into prepared pan. Score into squares while warm. When fudge is firm, use foil to lift it out of pan. Cut candy into squares. Store fudge tightly covered.

Truly an addiction, dark and creamy fudge is the most powerful fix for the confirmed chocoholic.

COFFEE CREAMS

PREP TIME: 45 MINUTES COOK TIME: 30 MINUTES STAND TIME: 1 HOUR

✳ In a heavy 1½-quart saucepan combine sugar, water, half-and-half or cream, coffee crystals, and corn syrup. Cook over medium heat, stirring constantly with a wooden spoon to dissolve sugar. Avoid splashing mixture on sides of pan.

✳ Carefully clip a candy thermometer to side of pan. Cook, stirring occasionally, to 234° to 240°, soft-ball stage, (20 to 25 minutes). Mixture should boil at a moderate, steady rate over surface. Remove from heat. Cool, without stirring, to 110°. Remove thermometer. Add vanilla; beat with a wooden spoon until mixture becomes very thick and just starts to lose its gloss (about 10 minutes).

✳ Immediately shape mixture into ¾-inch balls. Place on waxed paper. Let stand about 20 minutes or until dry.

✳ Meanwhile, quick-temper the chocolate.* Dip balls, one at a time, into tempered chocolate. Let excess chocolate drip off balls. Place on waxed paper. Let stand until chocolate is firm. Store in a tightly covered container at room temperature.

*NOTE: To quick-temper chocolate, combine chocolate pieces with 3 tablespoons shortening in a 4 cup glass measure. Pour very warm water (100° to 110°) into a large glass bowl to a depth of 1 inch. Place the measure inside the bowl of water. *Do not splash any water into the chocolate.* The water should only cover the bottom half of the measure containing the chocolate. Stir mixture constantly until completely melted and smooth (15 to 20 minutes). If water cools, remove measure and replace water in the bowl. Return measure to water and continue stirring. When melted, the chocolate is ready for dipping. Repeat warming process if chocolate cools and hardens.

Bite into these seemingly innocent chocolate candies and your mouth will encounter the most adult flavor of coffee cream.

2   cups sugar

½   cup water

¼   cup half-and-half or light cream

1   tablespoon instant coffee crystals

1   tablespoon light-color corn syrup

½   teaspoon vanilla

16   ounces semisweet or milk chocolate pieces

3   tablespoons shortening

MAKES 56 CANDIES

TRIPLE CHOCOLATE TRUFFLES

Like an actress who assumes a guise, chocolate changes to suit the mood—casual... sultry...elegant...mysterious...

12 ounces semisweet chocolate, coarsely chopped

1/2 of an 8-ounce package cream cheese, softened and cut up

4 teaspoons instant coffee crystals

1 teaspoon water

1 1/3 cups milk chocolate or semisweet chocolate pieces, or 8 ounces white baking bar

2 tablespoons shortening

2 ounces white baking bar, milk chocolate, or semisweet chocolate, coarsely chopped

MAKES 30 TRUFFLES

PREP TIME: 1 HOUR CHILL TIME: 1½ HOURS

✳ In a heavy medium saucepan cook and stir semisweet chocolate over very low heat. Remove from heat; stir in the cream cheese until combined. Stir together coffee crystals and water; add to the chocolate mixture and stir until smooth. Cover and chill about 2 hours or until firm.

✳ Line a baking sheet with waxed paper. Use 2 spoons to shape the truffle mixture into 1-inch balls; place on prepared baking sheet. Cover and chill for 1 to 2 hours or until firm.

✳ In a heavy medium saucepan cook and stir milk chocolate, semisweet chocolate, or white baking bar and shortening over low heat until melted and smooth. Remove from heat; cool to room temperature.

✳ Use a fork to dip truffles into chocolate mixture, allowing excess chocolate to drip back into saucepan. Return truffles to baking sheet; chill about 30 minutes or until firm.

✳ In a heavy small saucepan cook and stir the white baking bar or chocolate over low heat until melted and smooth. Drizzle over the tops of the truffles (Use white baking bar to drizzle over milk or semisweet chocolate truffles. Use milk or semisweet chocolate to drizzle over the white baking bar truffles.) Before serving, chill for a few minutes or until set.

✳ To store, place truffles in a tightly covered container in the refrigerator. Let stand at room temperature about 30 minutes before serving.

NOTE: Triple Chocolate Truffles and Champagne Truffles (page 9) shown, right.

Fudgy Brownies With Frosting

½ cup butter

3 ounces unsweetened chocolate, coarsely chopped

1 cup sugar

2 eggs

1 teaspoon vanilla

²/₃ cup all-purpose flour

¼ teaspoon baking soda

½ cup chopped nuts (optional)

1 recipe Chocolate-Cream Cheese Frosting (optional)

MAKES 16 BROWNIES

✳ In a medium saucepan melt butter and unsweetened chocolate over low heat, stirring constantly. Remove from heat; cool.

✳ Meanwhile, grease an 8×8×2- or 9×9×2-inch baking pan; set aside. Stir sugar into chocolate mixture in saucepan. Add the eggs, 1 at a time, beating with a wooden spoon just until combined. Stir in the vanilla.

✳ In a small mixing bowl stir together the flour and baking soda. Add flour mixture to chocolate mixture; stir just until combined. If desired, stir in nuts. Spread the batter into the prepared pan.

✳ Bake in a 350° oven, allowing 30 minutes for an 8-inch pan or 25 minutes for a 9-inch pan. Cool on a wire rack. If desired, frost with Chocolate-Cream Cheese Frosting.

CHOCOLATE-CREAM CHEESE FROSTING: In a saucepan melt ½ cup semisweet chocolate pieces over low heat, stirring constantly. Remove from heat; cool. In a small bowl stir together one 3-ounce package softened cream cheese and 2 to 4 tablespoons powdered sugar. Stir in melted chocolate until smooth.

Certain fantasies are better kept between lovers. Share these dreamy brownies with the one you love.

CREAM CHEESE BROWNIES

PREP TIME: 30 MINUTES BAKE TIME: 45 MINUTES CHILL TIME: 1 HOUR

✳ Line a 13 9 2-inch baking pan with foil, extending foil over edges of pan. Grease foil; set aside. In a heavy large saucepan cook and stir the chocolate and butter over low heat until chocolate is melted. Set aside to cool.

✳ In a large bowl beat 2 of the eggs with an electric mixer on medium speed until foamy. Add the 1¼ cups sugar, the water, and 1 teaspoon of the vanilla; beat about 5 minutes or until mixture is thick and lemon-colored. Beat in cooled chocolate mixture. Stir in the 1 cup flour, baking powder, salt, and the ¾ cup nuts. Spread half of the batter in prepared baking pan; set pan and remaining batter aside.

✳ In a medium mixing bowl beat cream cheese, the ⅔ cup sugar, remaining 2 eggs, the 2 tablespoons flour, the lemon juice, and the remaining 1 teaspoon vanilla with an electric mixer until smooth. Spread evenly over batter in pan. Spoon remaining batter evenly over cream cheese mixture. Swirl batter with a knife to marble. Bake in a 350° oven for 45 minutes. Cool on a wire rack. Spread Chocolate Glaze over cooled brownies or, if desired, top each serving with a small amount of glaze and a whole macadamia nut. Chill 1 hour or until glaze is set.

CHOCOLATE GLAZE: In a small saucepan cook and stir ⅓ cup whipping cream and 6 ounces finely chopped semisweet chocolate over low heat until the chocolate is melted.

Create a sassy come-hither brownie with a haunting combination of silken cream cheese, macadamia nuts, and chocolate.

8 ounces semisweet chocolate, chopped

3 tablespoons butter

4 eggs

1¼ cups sugar

⅓ cup water

2 teaspoons vanilla

1 cup all-purpose flour

1 teaspoon baking powder

¼ teaspoon salt

¾ cup chopped toasted macadamia nuts

1 8-ounce package cream cheese, softened

⅔ cup sugar

2 tablespoons all-purpose flour

1 tablespoon lemon juice

1 recipe Chocolate Glaze

32 whole macadamia nuts (optional)

MAKES 32 BROWNIES

BUTTERMILK BROWNIES WITH FROSTING

A whisper of cinnamon adds memorable flavor to elegantly layered brownies covered with smooth sour cream frosting.

1 cup butter

¾ cup granulated sugar

¾ cup packed brown sugar

3 eggs

¼ cup buttermilk

1 teaspoon vanilla

1⅓ cups all-purpose flour

½ teaspoon baking soda

½ cup finely chopped toasted pecans

5 ounces semisweet chocolate, melted and cooled

½ teaspoon ground cinnamon

1 recipe Sour Cream Frosting or sifted powdered sugar

Dark chocolate curls (optional)

MAKES 36 BROWNIES

PREP TIME: 20 MINUTES BAKE TIME: 30 MINUTES

✳ Grease a 13×9×2-inch baking pan; set aside. In a medium saucepan melt the butter over low heat; cool slightly. Stir in the granulated sugar and brown sugar. Add the eggs, 1 at a time, beating by hand just until combined. Stir in buttermilk and vanilla.

✳ Stir together flour and baking soda. Add flour mixture to egg mixture; stir just until combined. Divide batter into 2 equal portions (about 1¾ cups each). Stir pecans into 1 portion and spread this batter into the prepared pan.

✳ Bake in a 350° oven for 10 minutes. Meanwhile, stir the melted chocolate and cinnamon into the remaining batter; blend well. Spread the chocolate batter over the partially baked brownies. Continue baking brownies about 20 minutes more or until a wooden toothpick inserted in the center comes out clean. Cool on a wire rack. Frost brownies with Sour Cream Frosting or sift powdered sugar over the top. If desired, garnish with chocolate curls.

SOUR CREAM FROSTING: In a medium mixing bowl beat together ⅓ cup dairy sour cream, ¼ cup softened butter, and 1 teaspoon vanilla with an electric mixer on low speed until smooth. Gradually add 3 cups sifted powdered sugar, beating on low speed until smooth and spreadable. Makes 1½ cups.

"TREASURE THE LOVE YOU RECEIVE ABOVE ALL.
IT WILL SURVIVE LONG AFTER YOUR GOLD AND
GOOD HEALTH HAVE VANISHED."

-Og Mandino

CHOCOLATE PISTACHIO HEARTS

PREP TIME: 45 MINUTES CHILL TIME: 30 MINUTES BAKE TIME: 9 MINUTES

✳ In a medium saucepan combine the butter and brown sugar. Heat and stir over low heat until butter is melted. Remove saucepan from heat; stir in vanilla. Cool mixture 15 minutes. Stir in beaten egg, flour, and cocoa powder until combined. Stir in the ¾ cup pistachio nuts. Divide dough in half. Cover and chill about 30 minutes or until dough is easy to handle.

✳ On a lightly floured surface, roll half of dough at a time to ¼-inch thickness. Using a 2-inch heart-shape cookie cutter, cut out cookies. Place cookies 1 inch apart on an ungreased cookie sheet.

✳ Bake in a 350° oven about 9 minutes or until edges are firm. Transfer cookies to a wire rack; cool.

✳ In a small heavy saucepan heat and stir chocolate pieces and shortening over low heat until melted. Remove from heat. Dip half of each cookie into chocolate mixture; roll edges of cookie in ground pistachio nuts.

Is there anything more alluring than the curve of a shoulder uncovered? Do these "half-dressed" cookies offer the same appeal?

1	cup butter
²/₃	cup packed brown sugar
1	teaspoon vanilla
1	beaten egg
2¼	cups all-purpose flour
¼	cup unsweetened cocoa powder
¾	cup finely chopped pistachio nuts
¾	cup semisweet chocolate pieces
1	tablespoon shortening
½	cup ground pistachio nuts

MAKES ABOUT 48 COOKIES

CHOCOLATE MINT SHORTBREAD

*To engage all
your senses with pleasure, sit in
front of a roaring fire and
enjoy these butter mint cookies
with hot coffee.*

³/₄ cup butter

³/₄ cup sifted powdered sugar

¹/₄ cup unsweetened cocoa powder

¹/₄ teaspoon mint extract

1¹/₃ cups all-purpose flour

³/₄ cup miniature semisweet chocolate pieces

Chocolate-flavored and/or vanilla-flavor green candy coating, melted (optional)

Crushed striped round peppermint candies (optional)

MAKES 16 SHORTBREAD COOKIES

PREP TIME: 20 MINUTES CHILL TIME: 1 TO 2 HOURS BAKE TIME: 25 MINUTES

✳ In a large mixing bowl beat butter with an electric mixer on medium to high speed for 30 seconds. Add powdered sugar, cocoa powder, and mint extract; beat until combined. Beat in as much of the flour as you can with the mixer. Stir in remaining flour and chocolate pieces. If necessary, cover and chill dough for 1 to 2 hours or until easy to handle.

✳ On a lightly greased cookie sheet, pat the dough into a 9-inch circle. Using your fingers, press all around the outside edge of dough every ¹/₂ inch to make a scalloped edge. Using a fork, prick dough deeply with the tines to form 16 wedges.

✳ Bake in a 300° oven about 25 minutes or until edges are firm to the touch and center is set. Cool on cookie sheet for 2 minutes. With a long, sharp knife, cut shortbread into wedges along the perforations. Transfer wedges to a wire rack; cool.

✳ If desired, drizzle melted candy coating over cookies; immediately sprinkle with crushed candies.

Double Chocolate Chunk Biscotti

PREP TIME: 30 MINUTES   BAKE TIME: 35 MINUTES

✳ Grease a large cookie sheet; set aside. In a large mixing bowl beat butter with an electric mixer on medium speed for 30 seconds. Add sugar, cocoa powder, and baking powder; beat until combined. Beat in eggs. Beat in as much flour as you can. Stir in remaining flour. Stir in the 4 ounces white baking bar and the 3 ounces semisweet chocolate.

✳ Divide dough in half. Shape each half into a 9-inch-long roll. Place rolls 4 inches apart on prepared cookie sheet; flatten rolls slightly to 2 inches wide.

✳ Bake in a 375° oven for 20 to 25 minutes or until a wooden toothpick inserted near the centers comes out clean. Cool on cookie sheet on a wire rack for 1 hour. Using a serrated knife, cut each roll diagonally into ½-inch-thick slices. Lay slices, one cut side down, on an ungreased cookie sheet.

✳ Bake slices in a 325° oven for 8 minutes. Turn slices over and bake 7 to 9 minutes more or until slices are dry and crisp. (Do not overbake.) Transfer to a wire rack; cool.

✳ If desired, in a heavy small saucepan combine the shortening and the 2 ounces semisweet chocolate or white baking bar. Cook and stir over low heat until melted and smooth. Drizzle over tops of biscotti. Let stand until set. Store in an airtight container up to 1 week.

⅓ **cup butter**

⅔ **cup sugar**

¼ **cup unsweetened cocoa powder**

2 **teaspoons baking powder**

2 **eggs**

1¾ **cups all-purpose flour**

4 **ounces white baking bar, coarsely chopped**

3 **ounces semisweet chocolate, chopped**

2 **tablespoons shortening (optional)**

2 **ounces semisweet chocolate or white baking bar, coarsely chopped (optional)**

MAKES 32 BISCOTTI

Like a reticent lover coaxed under a spell, these cookies dissolve tenderly when immersed in coffee or cocoa.

Chocolate Cherry Cookies

1½ cups all-purpose flour

½ cup unsweetened cocoa powder

½ cup butter

1 cup sugar

¼ teaspoon baking soda

¼ teaspoon baking powder

¼ teaspoon salt

1 egg

1½ teaspoons vanilla

48 undrained maraschino cherries (about one 10-ounce jar)

1 6-ounce package semisweet chocolate pieces (1 cup)

½ cup sweetened condensed milk

MAKES 48 COOKIES

✳ Combine flour and cocoa powder; set aside. In a mixing bowl beat butter with an electric mixer until softened. Add sugar, baking soda, baking powder, and salt; beat until combined. Beat in the egg and vanilla. Gradually beat in flour mixture.

✳ Shape dough into 1-inch balls. Place on an ungreased cookie sheet. Press down center of each ball with thumb. Drain maraschino cherries, reserving juice. Place a cherry in the center of each cookie. For frosting, in a small saucepan combine chocolate pieces and sweetened condensed milk; heat until chocolate is melted. Stir in 4 teaspoons reserved cherry juice.

✳ Spoon about 1 teaspoon frosting over each cherry, spreading to cover cherry. (If necessary, thin the frosting with additional cherry juice.) Bake in a 350° oven about 10 minutes or until edges are firm. Cool on cookie sheet for 1 minute. Transfer to a wire rack; cool.

Uncover the allure of these beguiling cookies—a hidden burst of cherry flavor in every bite of pure pleasure.

WHITE CHOCOLATE RASPBERRY COOKIES

Ladylike at a tea, innocent pleasure at a child's party, or sinful at a grown-up moment, these cookies adapt to the occasion.

8 ounces white baking bar, coarsely chopped

1/2 cup butter

1 cup sugar

1 teaspoon baking soda

1/4 teaspoon salt

2 eggs

2 3/4 cups all-purpose flour

1/2 cup seedless raspberry jam

3 ounces white baking bar, coarsely chopped

1/2 teaspoon shortening

MAKES ABOUT 48 COOKIES

PREP TIME: 30 MINUTES   BAKE TIME: 7 MINUTES

✳ In a heavy small saucepan melt 4 ounces of the white baking bar over low heat, stirring constantly; cool. Lightly grease a cookie sheet; set aside.

✳ In a large mixing bowl beat butter with an electric mixer on medium to high speed about 30 seconds or until softened. Add sugar, baking soda, and salt; beat until combined. Beat in eggs and melted white baking bar until combined. Beat in as much of the flour as you can. Stir in remaining flour. Stir remaining 4 ounces of the chopped white baking bar into batter.

✳ Drop batter by rounded teaspoons 2 inches apart onto prepared cookie sheet. Bake in a 375° oven for 7 to 9 minutes or until cookies are lightly brown around edges. Cool on cookie sheet for 1 minute. Transfer cookies to a wire rack; cool. (If desired, make ahead and store in an airtight container for up to 3 days.)

✳ In a small saucepan heat and stir the jam over low heat until melted. Spoon about 1/2 teaspoon jam onto top of each cookie. In a small saucepan heat and stir the 3 ounces white baking bar and shortening over low heat until melted. Drizzle over each cookie. If necessary, to firm chocolate, chill cookies about 15 minutes.

Chocolate Chunk Cookies

PREP TIME: 30 MINUTES   BAKE TIME: 9 MINUTES

✳ Place unsweetened chocolate in a heavy small saucepan. Cook and stir over very low heat until chocolate is melted. Set aside to cool.

✳ In a large mixing bowl beat butter with an electric mixer on medium to high speed for 30 seconds. Add granulated sugar, brown sugar, baking soda, and cooled chocolate. Beat until combined, scraping sides of bowl. Beat in eggs and vanilla until combined. Gradually beat in flour. Stir in the white baking bar and chocolate, and, if desired, nuts.

✳ Drop by rounded tablespoons 3 inches apart on an ungreased cookie sheet. Bake in a 375° oven 9 to 11 minutes or until edges are firm. Cool on cookie sheet 1 minute. Transfer to a wire rack; cool.

2 ounces unsweetened chocolate, chopped

1 cup butter, softened

3/4 cup granulated sugar

3/4 cup packed brown sugar

1 teaspoon baking soda

2 eggs

1 teaspoon vanilla

2 cups all-purpose flour

6 ounces white baking bar, cut into 1/2-inch pieces

6 ounces semisweet or bittersweet chocolate, cut into 1/2-inch pieces

1 cup chopped black walnuts or pecans (optional)

MAKES ABOUT 45 COOKIES

These cookies fulfill sweet desires never imagined—chocolate in three ways—all at one time.

ULTIMATE CHOCOLATE COOKIES

Create the ultimate moment with the ultimate cookie. Lower the lights, spark the fire, and delight in the splendor.

1   12-ounce package (2 cups) semisweet chocolate pieces

2   ounces unsweetened chocolate

2   tablespoons butter

¼   cup all-purpose flour

¼   teaspoon baking powder
    Dash salt

2   eggs

⅔   cup sugar

1   teaspoon vanilla

1   cup chopped nuts

4   ounces semisweet chocolate, melted

MAKES ABOUT 36 COOKIES

PREP TIME: 20 MINUTES   BAKE TIME: 8 MINUTES

✳ Lightly grease a cookie sheet; set aside.

✳ In a heavy medium saucepan combine 1 cup of the chocolate pieces, the unsweetened chocolate, and butter. Cook and stir over low heat until melted. Transfer to a large mixing bowl; cool slightly. Meanwhile, stir together flour, baking powder, and salt; set aside.

✳ Add eggs, sugar, and vanilla to chocolate mixture. Using a wooden spoon, beat until combined. Add flour mixture; beat until combined. Stir in remaining chocolate pieces and the nuts. Drop dough by heaping teaspoons about 2 inches apart onto prepared cookie sheet.

✳ Bake in a 350° oven for 8 to 10 minutes or until edges are firm and surface is dull and cracked. Cool cookies on cookie sheet for 1 minute. Transfer to a wire rack; cool completely. Drizzle melted chocolate over cookies.

"THE SOUND OF A KISS
IS NOT SO LOUD AS THAT OF A CANNON, BUT ITS ECHO
LASTS A GREAT DEAL LONGER."

–Oliver Wendell Holmes

FROZEN TREATS

CHOCOLATE TRUFFLE DESSERT

Save this elegant, smooth, and decidedly decadent chocolate dessert for your most special times.

6 ounces bittersweet or semisweet chocolate, chopped

1 cup whipping cream

¼ cup Irish cream liqueur, coffee liqueur, amaretto, or milk

2 slightly beaten egg yolks

2 tablespoons sugar

Melted white and/or dark chocolate (optional)

White chocolate shavings (optional)

MAKES 4 TO 6 SERVINGS

PREP TIME: 25 MINUTES FREEZE TIME: 4 HOURS

✳ Line an 8×8×2-inch pan with plastic wrap, extending plastic wrap over edges of pan; set aside.

✳ In a heavy medium saucepan melt chopped chocolate over very low heat, stirring constantly until chocolate begins to melt. Remove from heat; stir until smooth.

✳ In a chilled mixing bowl combine the whipping cream and 1 tablespoon of the liqueur. Beat with an electric mixer on low speed until soft peaks form (tips curl). Cover; refrigerate up to 2 hours.

✳ In a heavy small saucepan stir together yolks, sugar, and remaining liqueur or milk. Cook over medium-low heat until thick (about 8 minutes), stirring frequently with a wire whisk. Remove from heat; pour into a medium bowl. Add melted chocolate, 2 tablespoons at a time, to hot yolk mixture, beating on medium speed until combined. Add ½ cup of whipped cream mixture; beat on low speed until smooth. Fold in remaining whipped cream. Spoon evenly into prepared pan. Cover; freeze about 4 hours or until firm.

✳ Line a baking sheet with waxed paper. Invert frozen chocolate mixture onto baking sheet. Remove plastic. Using 1-, 2-, and 3-inch star-shape cookie cutters, cut shapes from chocolate, dipping cutters into warm water between cuts. Cover; return shapes to freezer until serving time. To serve, if desired, drizzle plates with melted chocolate. Place frozen cutouts on chocolate drizzles and, if desired, sprinkle with white chocolate shavings.

CHOCOLATE PÂTÉ

This is the gold Krugerrand to chocolate lovers: chocolate in its creamiest, densest, and most opulent form.

6 ounces bittersweet or semisweet chocolate, chopped

1 cup whipping cream

2 tablespoons sugar

2 tablespoons milk

2 slightly beaten egg yolks

1 recipe Crème Anglaise or Raspberry Sauce (page 53)

MAKES 12 SERVINGS

PREP TIME: 40 MINUTES FREEZE TIME: 4 HOURS STAND TIME: 15 MINUTES

✳ In a small saucepan melt chocolate; set aside. Line the bottom and sides of a 7½×3½×2-inch loaf pan with plastic wrap, extending wrap over edges of pan; set aside.

✳ In a small chilled mixing bowl beat whipping cream with the chilled beaters of an electric mixer on low speed until soft peaks form (tips curl). Cover; refrigerate until needed.

✳ In another heavy small saucepan stir together sugar, milk, and egg yolks. Heat just until bubbly, stirring constantly. Remove from heat; pour mixture into a bowl. Gradually add melted chocolate to the hot mixture, beating on low speed until combined (mixture will be stiff). Add ½ cup of the whipped cream; continue beating on low speed until smooth. Gently fold in remaining whipped cream by hand. Spoon mixture into prepared pan. Cover and freeze at least 4 hours before serving.

✳ To serve, invert pâté onto a plate. Remove pan. Peel off plastic wrap. Let pâté stand 15 minutes. Using a hot, dry knife, cut into slices. Serve with Crème Anglaise or Raspberry Sauce.

CRÈME ANGLAISE: In a heavy small saucepan combine 1 beaten egg; ⅔ cup milk, half-and-half, or light cream; and 4 teaspoons sugar. Cook and stir over medium heat. Continue cooking egg mixture until it just coats a metal spoon. Remove pan from heat. Stir in ½ teaspoon vanilla. Quickly cool the custard by placing the saucepan into a sink of ice water for 1 to 2 minutes, stirring constantly. Cover surface with plastic wrap. Cool slightly. Chill until serving time. Makes 1 cup.

"LOVE LOOKS NOT WITH THE EYES, BUT WITH THE MIND; AND THEREFORE IS WINGED CUPID PAINTED BLIND."

—*William Shakespeare*

Candy Bar Terrine

PREP TIME: 1½ HOURS BAKE TIME: 20 MINUTES FREEZE TIME: OVERNIGHT

1 19½- to 22½-ounce package brownie mix

½ cup milk

2 cups tiny marshmallows

1½ 7-ounce bars milk chocolate (without almonds), broken (10 ounces total)

1 cup whipping cream

1 recipe Bittersweet Hot Fudge Sauce (page 86) or purchased chocolate ice cream sauce (optional)

MAKES 12 TO 14 SERVINGS

✳ For brownie, grease a 15×10×1-inch baking pan and line with waxed paper; grease and flour the waxed paper. Set pan aside. Prepare brownie mix according to package directions; pour batter into prepared pan. Bake in a 350° oven for 20 minutes. Cool in pan on a wire rack for 10 minutes; loosen edges and remove from pan. Cool completely on a wire rack.

✳ Meanwhile, for filling, heat milk in a saucepan over low heat until steaming, stirring constantly. Add marshmallows; stir until melted. Add broken chocolate bars; stir until melted. Remove from heat. Cover surface of chocolate mixture with waxed paper; cool to room temperature.

✳ In a chilled bowl beat the 1 cup whipping cream with chilled beaters on medium speed until soft peaks form (tips curl). Fold cooled chocolate mixture into whipped cream. Line two 7½×3½×2-inch loaf pans with plastic wrap. Cut brownie to fit the long sides and the bottom of pans. Line pans with brownie pieces, cutting to fit. (Do not line ends of pans with brownie.) Fill lined pans with cooled filling. Cover with additional brownie pieces. Cover with plastic wrap; freeze overnight.

✳ To serve, uncover and invert terrine onto a serving platter. Remove plastic wrap. Use a hot knife to slice terrine. Place 2 slices on each dessert plate. If desired, serve with hot fudge sauce or chocolate sauce.

Brownies and ice cream become as one—frozen together—in this irresistible chocolate-drizzled dessert.

CHOCOLATE-ALMOND ICE CREAM ROLL

PREP TIME: 30 MINUTES BAKE TIME: 12 MINUTES FREEZE TIME: 4 HOURS

✳ Grease and flour a 15¥10¥1-inch baking pan. In a bowl stir together flour, cocoa powder, baking powder, and salt. Set aside. In a small mixing bowl beat egg yolks and vanilla with an electric mixer on high speed about 5 minutes or until lemon-colored. Gradually add the ⅓ cup granulated sugar, beating on medium speed 5 minutes or until sugar is almost dissolved. Wash beaters.

✳ In a large mixing bowl beat egg whites on medium speed until soft peaks form (tips curl). Gradually add the ½ cup granulated sugar, beating on high speed until stiff peaks form (tips stand straight). Fold egg yolk mixture into beaten egg whites. Sprinkle flour mixture over egg mixture; fold in gently just until combined. Spread batter evenly into prepared pan.

✳ Bake cake in a 375° oven for 12 to 15 minutes or until top springs back when lightly touched. Immediately loosen edges of cake from pan; turn out onto a towel sprinkled with powdered sugar. Roll up towel and cake, starting from one of the short sides. Cool on a wire rack.

✳ Unroll cake; remove towel. Spread softened ice cream on cake to within 1 inch of edges. Roll up cake. Wrap in foil; freeze at least 4 hours.

✳ To serve, slice ice cream roll: place slices on dessert plates. Spoon Raspberry Sauce next to each slice. If desired, decorate sauce using melted white chocolate and garnish with raspberries.

Chocolate cake encases ice cream in a beautiful concentric swirl. Raspberry sauce adds to its charm.

⅓ cup all-purpose flour

¼ cup unsweetened cocoa powder

1 teaspoon baking powder

¼ teaspoon salt

4 egg yolks

½ teaspoon vanilla

⅓ cup granulated sugar

4 egg whites

½ cup granulated sugar

Sifted powdered sugar

1 quart butter-almond or chocolate-almond ice cream, softened

1 recipe Raspberry Sauce (page 53)

Melted white chocolate (optional)

Fresh raspberries (optional)

MAKES 10 SERVINGS

Irish Chocolate Ice Cream

PREP TIME: 20 MINUTES FREEZE TIME: 8 HOURS

✳ In a heavy medium saucepan combine the egg yolks, sugar, milk, half-and-half or light cream, chocolate, and coffee crystals. Cook and stir over medium heat until the mixture is slightly thickened and bubbly; remove from heat. Beat mixture with a rotary beater until smooth. Transfer to a medium bowl. Cool thoroughly by placing bowl in a sink or large bowl of ice water; stir occasionally. Stir in whiskey.

✳ In a large mixing bowl beat whipping cream with an electric mixer on medium speed until soft peaks form (tips curl). Fold in cooled chocolate mixture. Pour into an 8¥8¥2-inch baking pan. Cover and freeze at least 8 hours or overnight until firm. Let stand at room temperature for 10 to 15 minutes before serving.

4 beaten egg yolks

¾ cup sugar

¾ cup milk

¾ cup half-and-half or
    light cream

3 ounces semisweet chocolate,
    coarsely chopped

2 tablespoons instant coffee crystals

¼ cup Irish whiskey or bourbon
    whiskey

2 cups whipping cream

MAKES ABOUT 12 SERVINGS
(1 ½ QUARTS)

*Let the spirited coolness and
velvety smoothness of this ice cream caress your tongue.
Truly a sensual moment to savor.*

Triple Chocolate Ice Cream

PREP TIME: 45 MINUTES RIPEN TIME: 4 HOURS

4 ounces white baking bar, chopped

2 cups half-and-half or light cream

3/4 cup sugar

2 beaten egg yolks

3 cups whipping cream

1 tablespoon vanilla

2 ounces milk chocolate, chopped

2 ounces semisweet or bittersweet chocolate, chopped

MAKES ABOUT 16 SERVINGS (ABOUT 2 QUARTS)

✶ Melt white baking bar; cool. In a heavy large saucepan combine the half-and-half or light cream and sugar. Cook and stir over medium heat just until sugar is dissolved.

✶ Gradually stir about 1 cup of the warm mixture into beaten egg yolks. Return all of the egg yolk mixture to the saucepan. Bring to a gentle boil, stirring constantly. Remove from heat.

✶ Stir melted white baking bar into the egg yolk mixture until combined. Stir in whipping cream and vanilla. Cool thoroughly by placing the saucepan in a sink of ice water or chill overnight in the refrigerator.

✶ Stir milk chocolate and semisweet chocolate into the egg yolk mixture. Freeze in a 4- or 5-quart ice cream freezer according to the manufacturer's directions. Ripen 4 hours.

White, milk, and dark chocolate overpower your senses in this heady deluxe chocolate ice cream.

"...YOUR LOVE IS BETTER THAN CHOCOLATE..."

—Sarah McLachlan (from "Ice Cream")

PIES and PASTRIES

Berry Truffle Pie

PREP TIME: 40 MINUTES CHILL TIME: 4 HOURS STAND TIME: 30 MINUTES

＊ Prepare and/or bake pastry shell; set aside. In a saucepan combine chocolate and butter. Heat and stir over medium-low heat until melted. Add cream cheese and liqueur. Heat and stir until combined. Remove from heat. Stir in the powdered sugar. Spread in baked pastry shell. Arrange strawberries and mixed berries on filling, placing strawberries stem ends down. Melt jelly; brush over berries. Cover; chill for 4 hours.

＊ Let pie stand at room temperature for 30 minutes before serving. Beat whipping cream with the 2 tablespoons powdered sugar and the orange peel until soft peaks form. Spoon or pipe whipped cream into center of pie.

PASTRY FOR SINGLE-CRUST PIE: Stir together 1¼ cups all-purpose flour and ¼ teaspoon salt. Using a pastry blender, cut in ⅓ cup shortening until pieces are pea-size. Sprinkle 1 tablespoon cold water over part of mixture; gently toss with a fork. Push moistened dough to side of bowl. Repeat, using 1 tablespoon of water at a time, until flour mixture is moistened (4 to 5 tablespoons total). Form dough into a ball. On a floured surface, roll dough into a 12-inch circle. Ease dough into a 9-inch pie plate. Trim to ½ inch beyond edge of plate. Fold under extra dough. Crimp edge. Prick bottom and sides of pastry. Line with a double thickness of foil. Bake in a 450° oven 8 minutes. Remove foil. Bake 5 to 6 minutes more or until golden.

1 recipe Pastry for Single-Crust Pie or ½ of a 15-ounce package refrigerated piecrusts (1 crust)

1 6-ounce package (1 cup) semisweet chocolate pieces

1 tablespoon butter

1 8-ounce package cream cheese, softened

2 tablespoons orange liqueur

¼ cup sifted powdered sugar

1 quart whole strawberries, rinsed and stems removed

1 cup mixed berries, such as blueberries and raspberries

2 tablespoons red currant jelly

½ cup whipping cream

2 tablespoons sifted powdered sugar

½ teaspoon finely shredded orange peel

MAKES 8 SERVINGS

This satiny smooth pie, kissed with a hint of orange liqueur, is the perfect foil for plump, juicy berries of every kind.

WHITE CHOCOLATE AND COCONUT CREAM PIE

Relish the many intrigues of this opulent pie with crème de cacao whipped cream and a coconut custard filling.

2   cups coconut

1/2 cup crushed graham crackers

1/4 cup butter, melted

2   cups milk

6   egg yolks

3/4 cup granulated sugar

1/2 cup all-purpose flour

2   tablespoons butter

2   tablespoons crème de cacao

4   ounces white baking bar, chopped

2   cups whipping cream

1/2 cup sifted powdered sugar

1   tablespoon crème de cacao (optional)

    Toasted coconut or white baking bar curls (optional)

MAKES 8 SERVINGS

PREP TIME: 40 MINUTES   BAKE TIME: 10 MINUTES   CHILL TIME: 2½ HOURS

✳ For crust, stir together 1 cup of the coconut, the graham crackers, and melted butter. Press onto bottom and up sides of a 9-inch pie plate. Bake in a 350° oven for 10 minutes. Cool on a wire rack.

✳ For filling, in a large heavy saucepan heat milk and remaining coconut just to simmering, stirring occasionally.

✳ Meanwhile, in a mixing bowl combine egg yolks, granulated sugar, and flour. Beat with an electric mixer on medium-high speed until combined. Gradually stir 1 cup of the hot milk mixture into the egg yolk mixture. Return all of the yolk mixture to the saucepan. Cook and stir until mixture comes to boiling. Cook and stir for 2 minutes more. Remove saucepan from heat. Stir in 1 tablespoon of the butter and the 2 tablespoons crème de cacao. Cover surface with clear plastic wrap; cool.

✳ Meanwhile, in a small saucepan melt white baking bar with remaining 1 tablespoon butter over low heat, stirring constantly. Spread onto bottom and sides of cooled crust. Cool until white baking bar is firm. Pour filling into crust. Cover and chill pie for 2 to 4 hours.

✳ Thirty minutes before serving, in a chilled mixing bowl beat whipping cream, powdered sugar, and, if desired, the 1 tablespoon crème de cacao until stiff peaks form (tips stand straight). Swirl whipped cream over pie. Cover and chill for 30 minutes. If desired, garnish with coconut or white baking bar curls.

"YOU CANNOT TOUCH LOVE...BUT YOU FEEL THE SWEETNESS THAT IT POURS INTO EVERYTHING."

−Annie Sullivan

White Chocolate Cranberry Pie

PREP TIME: 1 HOUR CHILL TIME: UP TO 8 HOURS

1 recipe Pastry for Single-Crust Pie (page 42) or ½ of a 15-ounce package refrigerated piecrusts (1 crust)

1 16-ounce can whole cranberry sauce

2 tablespoons granulated sugar

1 tablespoon cornstarch

1 tablespoon cranberry liqueur

1½ cups white baking pieces

1 egg

2 tablespoons water

¼ teaspoon almond extract

2 cups whipping cream

2 tablespoons powdered sugar

1 teaspoon vanilla

MAKES 8 TO 10 SERVINGS

✳ Prepare and/or bake pastry shell; set aside. For cranberry filling, in a saucepan combine cranberry sauce, granulated sugar, and cornstarch. Cook and stir until boiling. Cook and stir 2 minutes more. Stir in liqueur; cool.

✳ For cream filling, in a heavy small saucepan melt white baking pieces over low heat, stirring constantly; remove from heat. Slightly beat egg and water. Gradually stir half of the melted pieces into egg mixture. Stir egg mixture into remaining melted pieces in pan. Cook and stir over medium heat about 7 minutes or until thickened. Remove from heat. Stir in almond extract; cool.

✳ In a mixing bowl beat cream, powdered sugar, and vanilla with an electric mixer on high speed until soft peaks form (tips curl); reserve half of whipped cream mixture for lattice top. Fold remaining whipped cream mixture into cooled egg mixture. Spoon half of the cream filling into the pastry shell.

✳ For drizzle, transfer ⅓ cup cranberry filling to a sieve set over a bowl; let drain. Set drained liquid aside; return cranberries to cranberry filling. Spread cranberry filling over cream filling in shell. Top with remaining cream filling. Fit a pastry bag with a large star tip; fill with reserved whipped cream mixture. Pipe a lattice on pie. If necessary, add a little water to drained cranberry liquid; drizzle over pie. Cover; chill up to 8 hours.

The stunning ruby color of the cranberry filling set against a lattice of white makes this pie showstoppingly gorgeous.

MERINGUE CRUST CHOCOLATE PIE

PREP TIME: 1½ HOURS BAKE TIME: 45 MINUTES CHILL TIME: 8 HOURS

✳ For meringue, combine egg whites, cream of tartar, and salt. Beat with an electric mixer on high speed until soft peaks form (tips curl). Gradually add sugar, beating until stiff peaks form (tips stand straight).

✳ Lightly spray a 9-inch pie plate with nonstick coating. Fill a pastry bag fitted with a large star tip with the meringue mixture. Beginning in the center and working in a spiral outward, pipe meringue over bottom and up sides of plate. (Or, use a spoon to spread meringue evenly into pie plate, building up sides.)

✳ Bake in the center of a 300° oven for 45 minutes or until lightly brown. Turn off oven. Let shell dry in the oven with the door closed at least 1 hour.

✳ For filling, in a small bowl soften gelatin in cold water. In a heavy medium saucepan combine 1 cup of the whipping cream, the semisweet chocolate, and unsweetened chocolate. Cook and stir over medium-low heat until chocolates melt and mixture is smooth. Remove from heat. Stir in softened gelatin mixture; stir in remaining whipping cream, mixing well. Transfer mixture to a large mixing bowl. Stir in vanilla. Place in a larger bowl of ice water, stirring occasionally, until chilled. (Or, cover and chill several hours or overnight.)

✳ Beat filling with an electric mixer on medium speed just until soft peaks form (do not overbeat). Mound filling into meringue shell. Cover and chill several hours or overnight. If desired, garnish top of pie with chocolate curls and strawberries.

Mounds of rich chocolate mousse piled high atop a cloudlike crust of meringue will make you weak in the knees.

3 egg whites

Dash cream of tartar

Dash salt

⅔ cup sugar

Nonstick spray coating

1 teaspoon unflavored gelatin

1 tablespoon cold water

3 cups whipping cream

8 ounces semisweet chocolate, chopped

1 ounce unsweetened chocolate, chopped

2 teaspoons vanilla

Chocolate curls (optional)

Strawberries (optional)

MAKES 10 SERVINGS

Triple Chocolate Silk Pie

PREP TIME: 20 MINUTES   COOL TIME: 30 MINUTES   CHILL TIME: 5 HOURS

✳ Prepare and/or bake pastry shell; set aside. For filling, in a heavy small saucepan melt chocolate over very low heat, stirring constantly until chocolate begins to melt. Immediately remove saucepan from the heat and stir until smooth; cool.

✳ In a medium mixing bowl beat sugar and butter with an electric mixer on medium speed about 4 minutes or until fluffy. Beat in melted chocolate and vanilla. Add egg product, ¼ cup at a time, beating on high speed after each addition and scraping the sides of the bowl constantly. Spoon the filling into the pastry shell. Cover and chill for 5 to 24 hours or until set.

✳ To serve, carefully spoon Semisweet Chocolate Topping into one side of a pastry bag fitted with a large star tip. Spoon White Chocolate Topping into other side. Pipe topping in small puffs over the top of pie.

SEMISWEET CHOCOLATE TOPPING: Melt 3 ounces chopped semisweet chocolate with ¼ cup whipping cream; cool. In a small bowl beat ¾ cup whipping cream with electric mixer on low speed until soft peaks form (tips curl). Add chocolate mixture; continue beating on low speed just until stiff peaks form (tips stand straight).

WHITE CHOCOLATE TOPPING: Melt 3 ounces chopped white baking bar with ¼ cup whipping cream; cool. In small mixing bowl beat ¾ cup whipping cream with an electric mixer on low speed until soft peaks form (tips curl). Add baking bar mixture. Continue beating on low speed just until stiff peaks form (tips stand straight).

1 recipe Pastry for Single-Crust Pie (page 42) or ½ of a 15-ounce package refrigerated piecrusts (1 crust)

4 ounces unsweetened chocolate, chopped

1 cup sugar

¾ cup butter

1 teaspoon vanilla

¾ cup refrigerated or frozen egg product, thawed

1 recipe Semisweet Chocolate Topping

1 recipe White Chocolate Topping

MAKES 10 SERVINGS

The ultra smoothness of silk has long been appreciated in lingerie. The allure of silken smoothness translates to food as well.

Chocolate Hazelnut Pie

PREP TIME: 30 MINUTES BAKE TIME: 8 MINUTES CHILL TIME: SEVERAL HOURS

¾ cup all-purpose flour

⅓ cup very finely chopped hazelnuts (filberts)

3 tablespoons brown sugar

⅓ cup butter, melted

1 8-ounce package cream cheese, softened

¾ cup semisweet chocolate pieces, melted and cooled

⅓ cup granulated sugar

2 tablespoons milk

1 cup whipping cream

1 cup frozen loose pack unsweetened red raspberries, thawed

2 tablespoons light-color corn syrup

¼ cup semisweet chocolate pieces

2 tablespoons butter

MAKES 10 SERVINGS

✳ In a small bowl combine flour, nuts, and brown sugar. Stir in melted butter; toss to mix. Press evenly onto the bottom and up sides of 9-inch pie plate. Bake in a 425° oven for 8 to 10 minutes or until brown; cool.

✳ For filling, in a large mixing bowl combine cream cheese, melted chocolate, granulated sugar, and milk. Beat with an electric mixer on medium speed until smooth. Wash beaters. In a chilled bowl beat whipping cream until soft peaks form (tips curl); fold into cream cheese mixture. Spread filling into cooled crust. Cover and chill several hours or overnight.

✳ For sauce, in a blender container or food processor bowl combine raspberries and corn syrup. Cover and blend until nearly smooth. If desired, press sauce through a sieve to remove the seeds.

✳ To serve, melt the ¼ cup chocolate pieces and 2 tablespoons butter; drizzle over pie. Serve raspberry sauce with pie.

Like satin on skin, chocolate and cream cheese are luxurious when combined—a divine experience to behold.

"I LOVE YOU, NOT ONLY FOR WHAT YOU ARE,
BUT FOR WHAT I AM WHEN I AM WITH YOU."

–Roy Croft

FUDGE CROSTATA WITH RASPBERRY SAUCE

PREP TIME: 30 MINUTES   BAKE TIME: 40 MINUTES

✳ Place one piecrust in a 10-inch tart pan with a removable bottom or a 9-inch pie plate; press onto bottom and up sides of pan. Trim edges if necessary.

✳ For filling, in a small saucepan melt chocolate pieces and 2 tablespoons of the butter over low heat, stirring constantly until smooth. In a medium bowl beat remaining 6 tablespoons butter with the ⅔ cup sugar until combined. Add almonds, 1 egg, egg yolk, and melted chocolate mixture; mix well. Spread chocolate mixture evenly over bottom of pastry-lined pan.

✳ For lattice top, cut second prepared crust into ½-inch-wide strips. Arrange strips in lattice design over chocolate mixture. Trim and seal edges. Beat egg white in a small bowl until foamy; gently brush over lattice. If desired, sprinkle with sugar.

✳ Bake in a 425° oven for 10 minutes; reduce oven temperature to 350°. Bake 30 to 35 minutes more or until crust is golden. (To prevent overbrowning, if necessary, cover edge of crust with foil after 15 to 20 minutes of baking.) Cool completely.

✳ To serve, cut into wedges. If desired, garnish with raspberries and mint leaves. Serve with Raspberry Sauce.

RASPBERRY SAUCE: In a blender container or food processor bowl cover and blend or process one 12-ounce package frozen lightly sweetened red raspberries (thawed) on high speed until smooth. Press through a strainer to remove seeds; discard seeds. In a small saucepan stir together the raspberry puree, ¾ cup sugar, and 1 teaspoon lemon juice. Bring mixture to boiling over medium-low heat. Boil for 3 minutes, stirring constantly. Transfer sauce to a bowl.

The chocolate layer that forms the filling of this pastry-topped crostata will haunt your senses long after it is gone.

1 15-ounce package refrigerated piecrusts (2 crusts)

1 6-ounce package (1 cup) semisweet chocolate pieces

½ cup butter

⅔ cup sugar

1 cup ground almonds

1 egg

1 egg yolk

1 egg white

Additional sugar (optional)

Fresh raspberries (optional)

Fresh mint (optional)

1 recipe Raspberry Sauce

MAKES 12 SERVINGS

CHOCOLATE CINNAMON TART

Cinnamon is chocolate's devoted partner—it enlivens and awakens chocolate's deeply sensual side, enhancing its flavor.

1 recipe Pastry for Single-Crust Pie (page 42)

1/4 cup sugar

2 tablespoons cornstarch

1/4 teaspoon ground cinnamon

2 cups half-and-half, light cream, or milk

3 ounces semisweet chocolate, chopped

1 slightly beaten egg

1 tablespoon butter

1 teaspoon vanilla

Whipped cream (optional)

Ground cinnamon (optional)

MAKES 10 SERVINGS

PREP TIME: 35 MINUTES   BAKE TIME: 13 MINUTES   CHILL TIME: 3 HOURS

✳ Prepare Pastry for Single-Crust Pie according to recipe on page 42, except ease into a 9- or 10-inch fluted tart pan with a removable bottom. Trim pastry even with rim of pan. Do not prick. Line pastry with a double thickness of foil. Bake in a 450° oven for 8 minutes. Remove foil. Bake pastry 5 to 6 minutes more or until golden; cool.

✳ Meanwhile, for filling, in a medium saucepan combine the sugar, cornstarch, and 1/4 teaspoon cinnamon. Gradually stir in the half-and-half, light cream, or milk. Stir in chocolate. Cook and stir over medium-high heat until thickened and bubbly. Cook and stir 2 minutes more. Remove from heat. Gradually stir about half of the hot mixture into the beaten egg. Return all of the egg mixture to the saucepan. Cook and stir until nearly bubbly, but do not boil. Reduce heat; cook and stir for 2 minutes more. Remove from heat. Stir in butter and vanilla.

✳ Pour hot filling into the baked tart shell. Cover and chill for 3 to 4 hours or until set. If desired, top each serving with whipped cream and sprinkle with cinnamon.

Chocolate Orange Tart

PREP TIME: 50 MINUTES   BAKE TIME: 20 MINUTES   CHILL TIME: SEVERAL HOURS

❋ Prepare the nut crust and set aside. For filling, in a small saucepan heat whipping cream to simmering. Remove from heat; whisk in chocolate until smooth. If desired, whisk in orange liqueur or brandy. Cool about 30 minutes or until filling begins to thicken but is still pourable.

❋ Spread marmalade over bottom of crust. Pour the chocolate filling over marmalade. Cover and chill for several hours or until filling is firm. If desired, garnish with whipped cream and candied orange zest curls.

ALMOND CRUST: Combine 1½ cups toasted blanched almonds and ¼ cup packed brown sugar. In a food processor bowl or blender container cover and process or blend a portion of the nut mixture at a time, until nuts are finely ground. Transfer to mixing bowl. Stir in ¼ cup all-purpose flour. Add ¼ cup melted butter, stirring until well combined. Press mixture onto the bottom and 1 inch up the sides of a 9-inch tart pan with removable bottom or a 9-inch springform pan. Bake in a 325° oven about 20 minutes or until golden and firm to the touch. Cool on a wire rack.

1 recipe Almond Crust

¾ cup whipping cream

6 ounces semisweet chocolate, chopped, or one 6-ounce package (1 cup) semisweet chocolate pieces

2 tablespoons orange liqueur or brandy (optional)

⅓ cup orange marmalade

Whipped cream (optional)

Candied orange zest curls (optional)

MAKES 10 TO 12 SERVINGS

Subtle, sophisticated flavors connect in exquisite harmony when rapturous orange joins with passionately rich chocolate.

NUT AND CHOCOLATE CHIP TART

✳ Prepare Pastry for Single-Crust Pie according to recipe on page 42, except ease pastry into an 11-inch tart pan with a removable bottom. Trim pastry even with the rim of the pan. Do not prick pastry.

✳ For filling, in a large mixing bowl beat eggs slightly with a fork. Stir in corn syrup. Add brown sugar, melted butter, and vanilla, stirring until sugar is dissolved. Stir in nuts and the ½ cup chocolate pieces. Place pastry-lined tart pan on a baking sheet on the oven rack. Pour filling into pan. Bake pie in a 350° oven about 40 minutes or until a knife inserted near the center comes out clean; cool.

✳ To serve, cut tart into wedges; transfer to dessert plates. If desired, in a small heavy saucepan melt the ⅓ cup chocolate pieces and shortening over very low heat. Immediately remove from heat; stir until smooth. Cool slightly. Transfer cooled chocolate to a small, heavy plastic bag. Snip a small hole in one corner of the bag. Place several drops of chocolate on each plate. Drag a wooden toothpick through each drop, creating a "tail." Or, drizzle chocolate over each serving. Cover and chill leftover tart for up to 2 days.

The addition of chocolate to a pecan pie filling creates a splendid dessert you won't soon forget.

1 recipe Pastry for Single-Crust Pie (page 42)

3 eggs

1 cup light-color corn syrup

½ cup packed brown sugar

⅓ cup butter, melted and cooled

1 teaspoon vanilla

1 cup coarsely chopped salted mixed nuts

½ cup miniature semisweet chocolate pieces

⅓ cup miniature semisweet chocolate pieces (optional)

1 tablespoon shortening (optional)

MAKES 8 TO 10 SERVINGS

CANDY CRÈME TART

Imagine all your favorite candies from childhood embedded in every creamy bite. It's a taste sensation that will make you smile.

PREP TIME: 25 MINUTES   BAKE TIME: 40 MINUTES   CHILL TIME: 4 HOURS

✳ For crust, stir together the crushed cookies, graham crackers, and the 1 tablespoon melted butter. Press crumb mixture onto the bottom and up the sides of a 9-inch tart pan with a removable bottom. Bake in a 350° oven for 10 minutes or until lightly brown. Set crust aside to cool.

✳ For filling, in a blender container or food processor bowl combine the cream cheese, the 3 tablespoons softened butter, half-and-half or light cream, eggs, sugar, and vanilla. Cover and blend or process until smooth. In a bowl stir together chopped candies. Stir into cream cheese mixture. Pour filling into crust-lined pan. Place in a shallow baking pan to catch any drips.

✳ Bake about 30 minutes or until center appears nearly set when shaken. Cool on a wire rack for 1 hour. Cover and chill at least 4 hours before serving.

³/₄ cup finely crushed shortbread cookies (about 12 cookies)

¼ cup graham cracker crumbs

1 tablespoon butter, melted

1 8-ounce package cream cheese, softened

3 tablespoons butter, softened

½ cup half-and-half or light cream

3 eggs

¼ cup sugar

1 teaspoon vanilla

3 1.4-ounce bars chocolate-covered English toffee, coarsely chopped

1 1.5-ounce bar white chocolate with chocolate cookie bits, coarsely chopped

15 malted milk balls, coarsely chopped

MAKES 12 SERVINGS

"THE BEST AND MOST BEAUTIFUL THINGS IN THE WORLD CANNOT BE SEEN OR EVEN TOUCHED. THEY MUST BE FELT WITH THE HEART."

–Helen Keller

Petite Chocolate Berry Pastries

1 package piecrust mix
(for 2 crusts)

¼ cup packed brown sugar

⅓ cup chocolate-flavor syrup

½ cup whipping cream

2 tablespoons granulated sugar

⅓ cup dairy sour cream

2 tablespoons orange liqueur

1½ cups raspberries, blackberries, blueberries, or sliced strawberries

Orange zest curls (optional)

Powdered sugar (optional)

MAKES 6 SERVINGS

PREP TIME: 25 MINUTES   BAKE TIME: 6 MINUTES   CHILL TIME: 4 TO 6 HOURS

✳ In a large mixing bowl combine pie crust mix and brown sugar; add syrup. Stir together until mixture forms a ball. On a lightly floured surface, roll dough to ⅛ inch thick. Using a 3-inch cookie or biscuit cutter, cut into rounds. Reroll trimmings as necessary to make 30 pastry rounds. Transfer rounds to an ungreased baking sheet. Bake in a 400° oven about 6 minutes or until set. Transfer to a wire rack and cool completely.*

✳ In a chilled mixing bowl combine the ½ cup whipping cream and granulated sugar. Beat with chilled beaters of an electric mixer on low speed until stiff peaks form. Fold in sour cream.

✳ To assemble each serving, top a pastry round with about 3 tablespoons of whipped cream mixture. Repeat layers. Place a third pastry on top. Cover with plastic wrap; chill 4 to 6 hours. (Chilling softens the pastry, making it easier to eat.)

✳ To serve, drizzle liqueur over berries; toss gently. Top each serving with additional whipped cream. Spoon some of the berries on top of each serving. If desired, garnish with orange zest curls and dust with powdered sugar.

*NOTE: Wrap and freeze any remaining pastry rounds for up to 6 months. Thaw at room temperature to serve.

Give the sour cream-laced whipped cream more panache—serve it billowing between layers of chocolate-flavored pastry.

CAKES
and
TORTES

CHOCOLATE WALNUT CAKE

> Like the homey warmth of a crackling fire on a wintry night, this cake envelops you in comfort.

$\frac{1}{2}$ cup unsweetened cocoa powder

$\frac{3}{4}$ cup boiling water

$\frac{1}{2}$ cup butter, softened

2 cups granulated sugar

1 8-ounce carton dairy sour cream

1 teaspoon vanilla

$\frac{1}{2}$ teaspoon baking soda

$\frac{1}{8}$ teaspoon salt

2 cups all-purpose flour

$\frac{1}{2}$ cup chopped walnuts

3 egg whites

$1\frac{1}{2}$ cups semisweet chocolate pieces

$\frac{1}{3}$ cup butter

$3\frac{1}{2}$ to 4 cups sifted powdered sugar

Semisweet chocolate and/or white baking bar curls (optional)

MAKES 16 SERVINGS

PREP TIME: 40 MINUTES   BAKE TIME: 35 MINUTES

✳ Grease and flour two 8×1½- or 9×1½-inch round baking pans; set aside. In a small bowl stir together cocoa powder and boiling water until smooth; cool 15 minutes.

✳ In a large mixing bowl beat the ½ cup butter with an electric mixer on medium to high speed for 30 seconds. Add granulated sugar and beat until combined. Add cocoa mixture, ½ cup of the sour cream, vanilla, baking soda, and salt; beat until combined. Using a spoon, stir in the flour and nuts.

✳ Wash beaters thoroughly. In a medium bowl beat egg whites until stiff peaks form (tips stand straight). Fold egg whites into the sour cream mixture. Pour batter into prepared pans.

✳ Bake in a 350° oven about 35 minutes for 8-inch pans or about 25 minutes for 9-inch pans or until a wooden toothpick inserted in centers comes out clean. Cool in pans on wire racks for 10 minutes. Remove cakes from pans. Cool thoroughly on wire racks.

✳ Meanwhile, for frosting, in a saucepan melt semisweet chocolate and the ⅓ cup butter over low heat, stirring frequently. Remove from heat; cool 5 minutes. Stir in the remaining sour cream. Gradually beat in enough of the powdered sugar to make frosting of spreading consistency.

✳ To assemble, place a cake layer, top side down, on a serving plate. Spread with about ⅔ cup frosting. Place the second cake layer, top side up, on top of the frosted layer. Frost top and sides with remaining frosting. If desired, garnish with chocolate curls. Store cake in the refrigerator.

"...WE ARE MADE FOR LOVING: ALL THE SWEETS OF LIVING ARE FOR THOSE THAT LOVE."

–Edward Fitzgerald

Cocoa Angel Cake

PREP TIME: 1 HOUR BAKE TIME: 40 MINUTES

✳ In an extra-large mixing bowl let egg whites stand at room temperature for 30 minutes. Meanwhile, sift the 1½ cups powdered sugar, the flour, and cocoa powder together 3 times; set aside.

✳ Add cream of tartar and vanilla to egg whites. Beat with an electric mixer on medium speed until soft peaks form (tips curl). Gradually add granulated sugar, 2 tablespoons at a time, beating until stiff peaks form. Sift about one-fourth of flour mixture over beaten egg whites; fold in gently. Repeat, folding in remaining flour mixture by fourths. Pour into an ungreased 10-inch tube pan. Using a knife, gently cut through batter to remove any large air pockets.

✳ Bake on the lowest rack in a 350° oven for 40 to 45 minutes or until the top springs back when lightly touched. Immediately invert the cake (leave in pan); cool thoroughly. Loosen sides of cake from pan; remove pan.

✳ For frosting, in a medium mixing bowl beat whipping cream with an electric mixer until soft peaks form (tips curl). Add the ¼ cup powdered sugar and beat until stiff peaks form (tips stand straight). Split cooled cake into 2 layers. Place a layer, top side down, on a serving plate. Spread with some of the frosting. Place second layer, top side up, on top of frosted layer. Frost top and sides with remaining frosting. If desired, top with chocolate curls and fresh raspberries.

1½ cups egg whites (10 to 12 large)

1½ cups sifted powdered sugar

1 cup sifted cake flour or sifted all-purpose flour

¼ cup unsweetened cocoa powder

1½ teaspoons cream of tartar

1 teaspoon vanilla

1 cup granulated sugar

1½ cups whipping cream

¼ cup sifted powdered sugar

Chocolate curls (optional)

Fresh raspberries (optional)

MAKES 12 SERVINGS

This angel food cake's sublime with the addition of cocoa. Truly a heavenly experience for the earthbound.

Mocha Truffle Roll

PREP TIME: 50 MINUTES   BAKE TIME: 12 MINUTES

⅓ cup all-purpose flour

¼ cup unsweetened
    cocoa powder

¼ teaspoon baking soda

¼ teaspoon salt

4 egg yolks

½ teaspoon vanilla

⅓ cup granulated sugar

4 egg whites

½ cup granulated sugar

Sifted powdered sugar

1 recipe Mocha Truffle Filling

Powdered sugar (optional)

MAKES 10 SERVINGS

✳ Grease and lightly flour a 15×10×1-inch baking pan. In a small bowl stir together flour, cocoa powder, baking soda, and salt; set aside.

✳ In a mixing bowl beat egg yolks and vanilla with an electric mixer on high speed 5 minutes or until lemon-colored. Gradually add ⅓ cup granulated sugar, beating until sugar is almost dissolved. Wash beaters. In another bowl beat egg whites on medium speed until soft peaks form. Add ½ cup granulated sugar, 2 tablespoons at a time, beating until stiff peaks form. Fold yolk mixture into whites. Sprinkle flour mixture over egg mixture; fold in gently just until combined. Spread batter evenly in prepared pan. Bake in 375° oven for 12 to 15 minutes or until cake springs back when lightly touched. Immediately loosen edges of cake; turn out onto a towel sprinkled with powdered sugar. Roll up cake and towel starting from one of the short sides. Cool on a rack. Unroll cake. Spread filling on cake to within 1 inch of edges. Reroll cake. Chill until serving time. Before serving, dust with powdered sugar.

MOCHA TRUFFLE FILLING: Dissolve 1 teaspoon instant coffee crystals in 2 tablespoons hot water. Beat ½ cup butter with an electric mixer on high speed until softened. Combine ½ cup unsweetened cocoa powder and 1½ cups sifted powdered sugar. Alternately add cocoa mixture and 3 tablespoons refrigerated egg product to butter, beating after each addition. Beat in coffee mixture, adding hot water, if necessary, to make of spreading consistency.

Creamy mocha filling oozes from the spiral of this chocolate truffle cake and teases your tongue.

DOUBLE FUDGE CAKE

PREP TIME: 35 MINUTES BAKE TIME: 40 MINUTES

✳ Grease a 13×9×2-inch baking pan. Combine flour, cocoa powder, baking soda, and salt; set aside.

✳ In a large mixing bowl beat shortening with an electric mixer on medium speed about 30 seconds or until softened. Add the 1 cup sugar and the vanilla; beat until combined. Add egg yolks, 1 at a time, beating well after each. Add flour mixture and water alternately to sugar mixture, beating on low to medium speed after each addition just until combined. Thoroughly wash beaters.

✳ In a large mixing bowl beat egg whites on medium to high speed until soft peaks form (tips curl). Gradually add the ¾ cup sugar, about 2 tablespoons at a time, beating until stiff peaks form (tips stand straight). Fold 2 cups of the cocoa batter into the egg white mixture to lighten. Gently fold cocoa-egg white mixture back into remaining batter until combined. Pour batter into prepared pan.

✳ Bake in a 350° oven about 40 minutes or until a wooden toothpick inserted in center comes out clean. Cool cake completely in pan on a wire rack. Frost with Fudge Frosting.

FUDGE FROSTING: In a medium saucepan combine one 5-ounce can evaporated milk, ½ cup sugar, and 2 tablespoons butter. Cook and stir over medium heat until milk mixture comes to boiling. Boil for 5 minutes, stirring occasionally. Remove pan from heat. Add 1½ cups semisweet chocolate pieces, stirring until melted. Add 1 tablespoon light-color corn syrup; stir until combined. Use frosting immediately.

Even the strongest become weak at the sight of the thick layer of outrageous fudge frosting on top of this chocolate cake.

2¼ cups all-purpose flour

½ cup unsweetened cocoa powder

1½ teaspoons baking soda

1 teaspoon salt

½ cup shortening

1 cup sugar

1 teaspoon vanilla

3 egg yolks

1⅓ cups cold water

3 egg whites

¾ cup sugar

1 recipe Fudge Frosting

MAKES 12 SERVINGS

White Chocolate Cake

PREP TIME: 45 MINUTES   BAKE TIME: 25 MINUTES

✳ Grease and lightly flour three 9×1½-inch round baking pans; set aside. In a large saucepan bring butter and water to boiling, stirring constantly. Remove from heat. Add baking bar; stir until melted. Stir in buttermilk, eggs, and rum extract.

✳ Stir together the ½ cup flour and the pecans; set aside. In an extra-large bowl stir together the 3 cups flour, the sugar, coconut, baking soda, and baking powder. Stir in egg mixture. Fold in pecan mixture. Divide batter among prepared pans.

✳ Bake in a 350° oven for 25 to 30 minutes or until a wooden toothpick inserted in the center comes out clean. Cool in pans on wire racks for 10 minutes. Remove cakes from pans. Cool cakes thoroughly on wire racks.

✳ To assemble, place a cake layer on a serving plate. Spread with ½ cup of White Chocolate Frosting. Repeat with second cake layer and another ½ cup frosting. Top with remaining cake layer. Frost top and sides with remaining frosting. If desired, cover cake with toasted coconut.

WHITE CHOCOLATE FROSTING: Melt 4 ounces chopped white baking bar; cool 10 minutes. Beat ½ cup softened butter and one 8-ounce and one 3-ounce package softened cream cheese with an electric mixer until combined. Beat in baking bar. Gradually add 6 cups sifted powdered sugar, beating until smooth.

1½   cups butter

¾   cup water

4   ounces white baking bar, chopped

1½   cups buttermilk

4   slightly beaten eggs

¼   teaspoon rum extract

½   cup all-purpose flour

1   cup chopped toasted pecans

3   cups all-purpose flour

2¼   cups sugar

½   cup flaked coconut

1   teaspoon baking soda

1   teaspoon baking powder

1   recipe White Chocolate Frosting

Toasted large flaked coconut (optional)

MAKES 16 SERVINGS

Like the glow of an angel, this cake's sweet radiance promises goodness within.

Cappuccino Decadence

½ cup finely crushed chocolate wafers

16 ounces semisweet chocolate, chopped, or 16 ounces (2⅔ cups) semisweet chocolate pieces

1 cup whipping cream

1 tablespoon instant coffee crystals

½ teaspoon ground cinnamon

6 beaten eggs

¾ cup granulated sugar

⅓ cup all-purpose flour

½ teaspoon finely shredded orange peel

Sifted powdered sugar (optional)

Whipped cream (optional)

Edible flowers, such as violets or pansies (optional)

MAKES 16 SERVINGS

✳ Grease a 9-inch springform pan. Lift and tilt the pan to coat the bottom and sides with crushed wafers; set pan aside.

✳ In a heavy medium saucepan combine chocolate, whipping cream, coffee crystals, and cinnamon. Cook and stir over low heat until the chocolate is melted. Transfer the hot mixture to a medium mixing bowl.

✳ In a large mixing bowl combine eggs, granulated sugar, and flour. Beat with an electric mixer on medium speed about 10 minutes or until thick and lemon-colored. Stir in orange peel. Fold one-fourth of the egg mixture into chocolate mixture. Fold chocolate-egg mixture into the remaining egg mixture. Pour into the crumb-coated pan.

✳ Bake in a 325° oven for 50 to 55 minutes or until edge is puffed and set about halfway to center (center will be slightly soft). Cool in pan on a wire rack for 20 minutes. Remove sides of pan; cool for 4 hours. Cover and chill at least 4 hours or until serving time. If desired, dust each serving with powdered sugar; top with whipped cream and edible flowers.

Like a first kiss, the sweet combination of coffee, cream, and chocolate is a thrill you won't forget.

FLOURLESS CHOCOLATE TORTE

PREP TIME: 35 MINUTES   BAKE TIME: 45 MINUTES   CHILL TIME: SEVERAL HOURS

✳ Grease bottom and sides of a 10-inch springform pan; set aside. Line a baking sheet with foil; set aside. In a heavy large saucepan combine the 1 pound chocolate, the butter, 1 cup whipping cream, and sugar. Cook and stir over medium-low heat until chocolate and butter are melted; remove from heat.

✳ In a large bowl whisk eggs and vanilla together. Slowly stir half of the chocolate mixture into egg mixture. Return egg mixture to remaining chocolate mixture, stirring until combined. Pour batter into prepared pan. Place pan on the lined baking sheet; place on oven rack.

✳ Bake in a 350° oven for 45 to 50 minutes or until evenly puffed and a knife inserted near center comes out clean. Remove from oven; cool thoroughly on a wire rack. Chill several hours or until firm. Set torte on a serving plate. Use a small metal spatula to loosen torte from sides of pan; remove sides of pan.

✳ In a small saucepan heat the 1 cup whipping cream just to boiling. Place the 12 ounces chocolate in a medium bowl. Add hot whipping cream; stir until chocolate is melted. Cool to room temperature. Spread over top of torte, allowing some of the mixture to drizzle down sides. Cover and chill for several minutes or until set.

✳ If desired, drizzle torte with melted milk chocolate. Let stand 30 minutes at room temperature before slicing.

Don't underestimate the power of this intense torte— just a sliver will excite your tastebuds, sending shivers down your spine.

1   **pound semisweet chocolate, cut up**

1   **pound butter**

1   **cup whipping cream**

1   **cup sugar**

9   **eggs**

4   **teaspoons vanilla**

1   **cup whipping cream**

12 **ounces semisweet chocolate, cut up**

1   **ounce milk chocolate, melted (optional)**

MAKES 16 TO 20 SERVINGS

BITTERSWEET CHOCOLATE TORTE

Raspberries and chocolate—two flavors that were meant for each other, just like Bogie and Bacall.

14 ounces bittersweet or semisweet chocolate, coarsely chopped

½ cup butter

¼ cup milk

5 eggs

1 teaspoon vanilla

½ cup granulated sugar

¼ cup all-purpose flour

¼ cup seedless red raspberry jam

1½ to 2 cups fresh raspberries

Sifted powdered sugar (optional)

MAKES 16 SERVINGS

PREP TIME: 30 MINUTES BAKE TIME: 30 MINUTES CHILL TIME: 8 HOURS

✳ Grease the bottom of an 8-inch heart-shape cake pan with a removable bottom or an 8-inch round springform pan; set pan aside. In a heavy medium saucepan combine chocolate, butter, and milk. Cook and stir over low heat until chocolate is melted. Remove from heat; cool mixture for 20 minutes.

✳ In a mixing bowl beat eggs and vanilla with an electric mixer on low speed until combined. Add granulated sugar and flour; beat on high speed for 10 minutes. Stir chocolate mixture into egg mixture. Pour batter into prepared pan.

✳ Bake in a 325° oven for 30 minutes (35 minutes for springform pan) or until outer one-third of top is slightly puffed. (Because this torte is so dense, you're unable to use a traditional cake doneness test. The torte should be done after 30 minutes, even though the center will still appear to be underbaked.)

✳ Cool torte on a wire rack for 20 minutes. Use a knife dipped in warm water to loosen torte from sides of pan. Cool torte thoroughly. Remove sides of pan. Wrap torte in foil; chill overnight or up to 2 days.

✳ To serve, bring torte to room temperature. In a small saucepan melt jam; cool. Spread jam on top of torte. Cover jam with raspberries, stem sides down. If desired, before serving, dust with powdered sugar.

Creamy Chocolate Cheesecake

PREP TIME: 2 HOURS   BAKE TIME: 45 MINUTES   CHILL TIME: 4 HOURS

1½ cups finely crushed chocolate wafers (about 27 cookies)

⅓ cup butter

4 ounces semisweet chocolate, chopped

3 8-ounce packages cream cheese, softened

¾ cup sugar

½ cup dairy sour cream

2 teaspoons vanilla

2 tablespoons all-purpose flour

3 eggs

1 recipe Chocolate Leaves (page 78) (optional)

MAKES 16 SERVINGS

✳ For crust, combine crushed wafers and butter. Press evenly onto the bottom and 1¾ inches up sides of a 9-inch springform pan. Set aside.

✳ For filling, in a heavy saucepan melt chocolate over low heat. Remove from heat; cool. In a medium mixing bowl beat together cream cheese, sugar, sour cream, and vanilla with an electric mixer on medium speed until smooth. Add flour; beat well. Add the cooled chocolate. Add the eggs all at once, beating on low speed just until combined.

✳ Pour filling into crust-lined pan. Place pan in a shallow baking pan on the oven rack. Bake in a 375° oven for 45 to 50 minutes or until center appears nearly set when shaken (center will look soft but will set up as it cools).

✳ Cool cheesecake in pan on a wire rack for 15 minutes. Use a small metal spatula to loosen crust from sides of pan. Cool 30 minutes more. Remove sides of pan. Cool 1 hour. Cover; chill at least 4 hours. If desire, garnish with Chocolate Leaves.

Ah, ecstasy reaches new heights when the creamy smooth texture of this cheesecake melts in your mouth.

WHITE CHOCOLATE CHEESECAKE

PREP TIME: 2 HOURS   BAKE TIME: 35 MINUTES   CHILL TIME: 4 HOURS

✳ For crust, combine crushed wafers and melted butter. Press evenly onto bottom and 2 inches up sides of a 9-inch springform pan; set aside.

✳ For filling, in a large mixing bowl beat cream cheese, sugar, flour, and almond extract or vanilla with an electric mixer on medium speed until combined. Add egg yolks and whole egg all at once, beating on low speed just until combined. Stir in half-and-half or light cream and white baking bar.

✳ Pour filling into the crust-lined pan. Place pan in a shallow baking pan on the oven rack. Bake in a 375° oven for 35 to 40 minutes or until center appears nearly set when shaken (the center will look soft but will set up as it cools).

✳ Cool cheesecake in springform pan on a wire rack for 15 minutes. Use a small metal spatula to loosen the crust from sides of pan. Cool 30 minutes more. Remove the sides of the pan. Cool cheesecake for 1 hour. Cover and chill at least 4 hours. If desired, garnish with white baking bar and milk chocolate curls.

Chiaroscuro is the art of light against dark; this white chocolate cheesecake, with its dark chocolate crust, mimics a work of art.

1¾   cups finely crushed chocolate wafers (about 33 cookies)

⅓   cup butter, melted

3   8-ounce packages cream cheese, softened

1   cup sugar

2   tablespoons all-purpose flour

½   teaspoon almond extract or vanilla

2   egg yolks

1   egg

¼   cup half-and-half or light cream

1   6-ounce package white baking bar, chopped

White baking bar and milk chocolate curls (optional)

MAKES 16 SERVINGS

CHOCOLATE RASPBERRY CHEESECAKE

This threesome will not raise eyebrows: Raspberry, chocolate, and almonds create a wonderful trio of flavors.

1 teaspoon butter

1 cup ground almonds

1 pound milk chocolate, chopped

4 8-ounce packages cream cheese, softened

½ cup butter, softened

⅓ cup milk

2 tablespoons raspberry liqueur, amaretto, or milk

4 eggs

1 egg yolk

1 recipe Chocolate Leaves (optional)

Fresh raspberries (optional)

MAKES 16 SERVINGS

PREP TIME: 2 HOURS BAKE TIME: 55 MINUTES CHILL TIME: 4 HOURS

✳ Grease the bottom of a 9-inch springform pan with the 1 teaspoon butter. Press almonds onto bottom of pan; set aside. Melt the chocolate in a heavy saucepan over very low heat, stirring constantly; cool.

✳ For filling, in a large mixing bowl beat melted chocolate, cream cheese, the ½ cup butter, milk, and liqueur or milk with an electric mixer on medium to high speed until combined. Add eggs and egg yolk all at once, beating on low speed just until combined. Pour filling into pan. Place pan in a shallow baking pan on the oven rack. Bake in a 350° oven about 55 minutes or until the center appears nearly set when shaken (center will look soft but will set up as it cools).

✳ Cool cheesecake in springform pan on a wire rack for 15 minutes. Use a small metal spatula to loosen cheesecake from sides of pan. Cool 30 minutes more. Remove sides of pan. Cool 1 hour. Cover; chill at least 4 hours. To serve, if desired, garnish with Chocolate Leaves and berries.

CHOCOLATE LEAVES: Melt 1 ounce semisweet chocolate. Using a small, clean paintbrush, brush melted chocolate on undersides of nontoxic leaves (such as lemon, lime, or mint). Wipe away any chocolate from top side of leaves. Place leaves, chocolate side up, on a curved surface. Let stand until firm. Carefully peel leaf from chocolate.

"TIME FLIES, SUNS RISE,
AND SHADOWS FALL—LET THEM GO BY,
FOR LOVE IS OVER ALL."

–Anonymous

Lava Baby Cakes

PREP TIME: 45 MINUTES   BAKE TIME: 13 MINUTES

✳ For filling, in a heavy small saucepan combine the ¾ cup chocolate pieces and whipping cream. Cook and stir over low heat until chocolate melts. Remove pan from heat. Cool, stirring occasionally. Chill until firm or for 30 to 45 minutes. Meanwhile, in a heavy medium saucepan cook and stir butter and the 1 cup chocolate pieces over low heat until melted. Remove from heat; cool.

✳ Form chilled filling into 6 equal-size balls; set aside. Lightly grease and flour six ¾-cup soufflé dishes or 6-ounce custard cups. Place dishes or cups in a 15×10×1-inch baking pan; set aside.

✳ In a mixing bowl beat eggs, egg yolks, granulated sugar, and vanilla with an electric mixer on high speed 5 minutes or until lemon-colored. Beat in chocolate-butter mixture on medium speed. Sift flour and cocoa powder over mixture; beat on low speed just until combined. Fill prepared dishes with about ⅓ cup batter. Place 1 ball of filling into each dish. Spoon remaining batter into dishes. (To make ahead, after filling dishes, cover and chill until ready to bake or up to 4 hours. Let stand at room temperature 30 minutes before baking.)

✳ Bake in a 400° oven about 13 minutes or until cakes feel firm at edges. Cool in dishes 2 to 3 minutes. Using a knife, loosen cakes from sides of dishes. Invert onto dessert plates. If desired, dust with powdered sugar; serve with Chocolate Whipped Cream or ice cream.

¾ cups semisweet chocolate pieces

2 tablespoons whipping cream

¾ cup butter

6 ounces (1 cup) semisweet chocolate pieces

3 eggs

3 egg yolks

⅓ cup granulated sugar

1½ teaspoons vanilla

⅓ cup all-purpose flour

3 tablespoons unsweetened cocoa powder

Powdered sugar (optional)

1 recipe Chocolate Whipped Cream (page 82) or coffee ice cream (optional)

MAKES 6 SERVINGS

A pool of chocolate spills onto your plate when you cut into these cakes—each bite is a sensual exploration of textures.

Chocolate Pound Cake

PREP TIME: 40 MINUTES BAKE TIME: 1½ HOURS

4 cups all-purpose flour

3 cups sugar

1 tablespoon baking powder

1½ teaspoons baking soda

½ teaspoon salt

2½ cups milk

1½ cups butter, softened

8 ounces unsweetened chocolate, melted and cooled

5 eggs

1 teaspoon vanilla

½ teaspoon almond extract

1 recipe Chocolate Whipped Cream

Toasted sliced almonds (optional)

MAKES 16 TO 20 SERVINGS

✳ Grease and lightly flour a 10-inch tube pan; set pan aside.

✳ In an extra-large mixing bowl combine flour, sugar, baking powder, baking soda, and salt. Add milk, butter, and melted chocolate. Beat with an electric mixer on low to medium speed until combined. Beat on medium speed for 2 minutes. Add eggs, vanilla, and almond extract. Beat 2 minutes more. Pour batter into the prepared pan, spreading evenly. Use a knife to cut a zigzag pattern through batter to break up any large air bubbles.

✳ Bake in a 325° oven for 1½ to 1¾ hours or until a wooden toothpick inserted in the center comes out clean. Cool in pan on a wire rack for 20 minutes. Remove cake from pan. Cool completely on wire rack. Serve slices with Chocolate Whipped Cream. If desired, sprinkle with toasted sliced almonds.

CHOCOLATE WHIPPED CREAM: In a heavy saucepan combine ¼ cup whipping cream and 3 ounces chopped bittersweet or semisweet chocolate. Heat over low heat, stirring constantly, until chocolate begins to melt. Remove from heat. Stir until smooth; cool. In a small mixing bowl beat ¾ cup whipping cream with an electric mixer on low speed just until soft peaks form. Add melted chocolate mixture. Continue beating on low just until stiff peaks form.

Chocolate Pound Cake, adorned with chocolate whipped cream, will be appropriately dressed for any setting—casual or elegant.

DOUBLE CHOCOLATE LOAF

PREP TIME: 25 MINUTES BAKE TIME: 1 HOUR

✳ Grease the bottom and ½ inch up the sides of an 8×4×2-inch loaf pan; set pan aside.

✳ In a medium mixing bowl combine flour, cocoa powder, baking powder, baking soda, and salt; set aside.

✳ In a large mixing bowl beat the butter with an electric mixer on medium speed for 30 seconds. Add sugar; beat until fluffy. Add eggs; beat until well combined. Add the flour mixture and buttermilk alternately to egg mixture, beating after each addition just until combined. Stir in nuts. Spoon half of the batter into the prepared pan. Sprinkle with chocolate pieces. Spoon on remaining batter.

✳ Bake in a 350° oven for 60 to 65 minutes or until a wooden toothpick inserted near center comes out clean. Cool in pan on a wire rack for 10 minutes. Remove cake from pan. Cool on a wire rack.

The best things in life are those that take you by surprise—like the ribbon of chocolate you'll find in every bite of this cake.

1²/₃ cups all-purpose flour

²/₃ cup unsweetened cocoa powder

½ teaspoon baking powder

½ teaspoon baking soda

½ teaspoon salt

½ cup butter, softened

1 cup sugar

2 eggs

1 cup buttermilk

¹/₃ cup chopped pecans or walnuts

¹/₄ cup miniature semisweet chocolate pieces

MAKES 10 SERVINGS

SAUCES

and

MORE

BITTERSWEET HOT FUDGE SAUCE

Some dangerous liaisons, like hot bittersweet fudge sauce and ice cold vanilla ice cream, are definitely worth the risk.

24	ounces semisweet chocolate, coarsely chopped
8	ounces unsweetened chocolate, coarsely chopped
3½	cups half-and-half or light cream
1¾	cups sugar
1	teaspoon vanilla
	Vanilla ice cream

MAKES EIGHT ½ PINTS

PREP TIME: 45 MINUTES

✳ In a 4-quart Dutch oven combine the chocolates, half-and-half or light cream, and sugar. Bring to boiling; reduce heat. Simmer mixture, uncovered, over low heat about 2 minutes or until mixture is creamy, stirring frequently. Remove from heat; stir in the vanilla.

✳ Pour the hot sauce into 7 or 8 hot, clean half-pint jars or 16 (4-ounce) jars, leaving a ½-inch headspace. Place metal lids on jars. Screw metal bands onto jars following manufacturer's directions. Store chocolate sauce in the refrigerator for up to 3 weeks. (The sauce must be stored in the refrigerator after placing in jars. Even though the hot sauce may cause the lids on the jars to seal, this is not a secure canning seal. Do not store at room temperature.) Serve sauce warm* over ice cream, éclairs, or fresh berries. Makes eight ½-pint or sixteen ½-cup jars.

SPIRITED HOT FUDGE SAUCE: Prepare sauce as directed, except use 32 ounces semisweet chocolate and decrease the half-and-half or light cream to 2 cups. Stir in ½ cup cherry, chocolate-mint, hazelnut, or orange liqueur with the vanilla. Makes seven ½-pint or fourteen ½-cup jars.

*NOTE: To reheat, place ½ cup sauce in a 1-cup glass measure. Microwave, uncovered, on 100% power (high) for 1½ to 2 minutes or until heated through, stirring once. Or, place in a small saucepan. Cook and stir over medium heat about 5 minutes or until heated through.

Chocolate Éclairs

PREP TIME: 35 MINUTES   BAKE TIME: 33 MINUTES

1 cup all-purpose flour

3 tablespoons unsweetened cocoa powder

2 tablespoons sugar

1 cup water

½ cup butter

¼ teaspoon salt

4 eggs

4 cups whipped cream

1 recipe Bittersweet Hot Fudge Sauce (page 86) or purchased hot fudge sauce (optional)

Powdered sugar (optional)

MAKES 12 ÉCLAIRS

✳ Grease a cookie sheet; set aside. Stir together flour, cocoa powder, and sugar. In a saucepan bring water, butter, and salt to boiling; stir until butter melts. Add flour mixture all at once to boiling mixture, stirring vigorously. Cook and stir until mixture forms a ball. Cool 10 minutes.

✳ Add eggs, one at a time, beating with a wooden spoon about 1 minute after each addition or until smooth.

✳ Spoon the batter into a pastry bag fitted with a large plain round tip (½- to 1-inch opening). Pipe strips of batter (measuring about 4 inches long, 1 inch wide, and ¾ inch high) 3 inches apart onto prepared cookie sheet.

✳ Bake in a 400° oven for 33 to 35 minutes or until puffy. Remove from cookie sheet; cool on a wire rack.

✳ Up to 2 hours before serving, cut off tops of éclairs. Remove soft dough from inside. Pipe whipped cream into éclairs. Replace tops. Chill until serving time. If desired, top with Bittersweet Hot Fudge Sauce and dust with powdered sugar.

Throw inhibitions aside as you unveil these naughty cream-filled chocolate pastries at your next dinner party for two.

CHOCOLATE FONDUE

✳ In a heavy medium saucepan melt chocolate over low heat, stirring constantly. Stir in sweetened condensed milk and milk; heat through. Transfer to a fondue pot; keep warm over a fondue burner.

✳ Serve fondue sauce immediately with assorted dippers. Swirl pieces as you dip. If the fondue mixture thickens, stir in some additional milk.

MOCHA FONDUE: Prepare as directed above, except substitute ⅓ cup strong coffee for the milk.

CHOCOLATE-PEANUT FONDUE: Prepare as directed above, except stir ½ cup creamy peanut butter in with the milk.

CHOCOLATE-LIQUEUR FONDUE: Prepare as directed above, except stir 2 to 4 tablespoons amaretto or orange, hazelnut, or cherry liqueur into mixture after heating.

Drenched in rich dark chocolate, any succulent strawberry or bite of brownie sweetens to irresistible proportions.

8 ounces semisweet chocolate, coarsely chopped

1 14-ounce can (1¼ cups) sweetened condensed milk

⅓ cup milk

Assorted dippers, such as angel food or pound cake cubes, brownie squares, marshmallows, dried apricots, whole strawberries, banana slices, or pineapple chunks

MAKES 8 SERVINGS

Chocolate Pots de Crème

PREP TIME: 15 MINUTES CHILL TIME: 2 HOURS

✳ In a heavy small saucepan combine the half-and-half or light cream, chocolate, and sugar. Cook and stir over medium heat about 10 minutes or until mixture reaches a full boil and thickens.

✳ Gradually stir about half of the hot mixture into the beaten egg yolks. Return all of the egg yolk mixture to the saucepan. Cook and stir over low heat for 2 minutes. Remove from heat; stir in vanilla. Pour chocolate mixture into 4 or 6 pots de crème cups or small dessert bowls. Cover and chill for 2 to 24 hours. If desired, top with Caramelized Shards.

CARAMELIZED SHARDS: Preheat oven to 350°. Line a cookie sheet with aluminum foil; coat foil with nonstick cooking spray. Sprinkle 1 tablespoon slivered almonds onto prepared foil. Bake in preheated oven 6 to 8 minutes or until lightly toasted. Meanwhile, place ⅓ cup sugar in a heavy 10-inch skillet. Heat over medium-high heat until sugar begins to melt, shaking skillet occasionally to heat sugar evenly. Do not stir. When sugar beings to melt, reduce heat to low. Cook for 2 minutes more or until sugar is melted and lightly golden, stirring as needed with a wooden spoon. Remove pan from heat. Stir in ½ teaspoon hot water. Immediately pour over nuts on hot baking sheet. Let cool for 1 minute. Using 2 forks, gently pull caramel as thinly as possible, lifting up slightly as you pull. Let cool thoroughly on foil. Break into pieces; store tightly covered.

1 cup half-and-half or light cream

1 4-ounce package sweet baking chocolate, coarsely chopped

2 teaspoons sugar

3 slightly beaten egg yolks

½ teaspoon vanilla
   Carmelized Shards (optional)

MAKES 4 TO 6 SERVINGS

Have a scandalous love affair with these little pots of cream. No one will think any less of you for doing so.

Chocolate Crème Brûlées

PREP TIME: 25 MINUTES BAKE TIME: 25 MINUTES CHILL TIME: UP TO 6 HOURS

2 cups whipping cream

3 ounces semisweet or bittersweet chocolate, chopped

6 slightly beaten egg yolks

¼ cup sugar

1 teaspoon vanilla

¼ teaspoon salt

3 tablespoons sugar

MAKES 6 SERVINGS

✳ In a heavy medium saucepan heat and stir the 2 cups whipping cream and chocolate over low heat until chocolate is melted. Remove from heat.

✳ In a large mixing bowl stir together egg yolks, the ¼ cup sugar, vanilla, and salt. Using a wire whisk, gradually stir hot cream mixture into egg yolk mixture.

✳ Place six ½-cup ramekins in a baking pan; set pan on oven rack. Pour egg mixture into ramekins. Pour boiling water or very hot water into baking pan around the ramekins to a depth of 1 inch. Bake in a 325° oven for 25 to 30 minutes or until a knife inserted near centers comes out clean. Remove ramekins from pan with water. Cool slightly on a wire rack.

✳ Immediately place the 3 tablespoons sugar in a heavy small skillet. Cook over medium-high heat until sugar just begins to melt, shaking skillet occasionally to heat evenly. (Do not stir.) Reduce heat to low. Cook and stir until sugar is melted and golden (watch closely, as sugar melts quickly). Drizzle about 1 teaspoon of melted sugar over each brûlée. Cool about 1 hour before serving. (Or, cool slightly. Do not drizzle with melted sugar. Cover and chill up to 6 hours. Let stand at room temperature 1 hour before serving. Drizzle with melted sugar before serving.)

Anyone with a burning passion for this little French number will adore the caramel-kissed chocolate custard. Ooh la la!

"THE HEART THAT LOVES IS ALWAYS YOUNG."

–Greek Proverb

RECIPE INDEX

Metric Cooking Hints

By making a few conversions, cooks in Australia, Canada, and the United Kingdom can use the recipes in this book with confidence. The charts on this page provide a guide for converting measurements from the U.S. customary system, which is used throughout this book, to the imperial and metric systems. There also is a conversion table for oven temperatures to accommodate the differences in oven calibrations.

Product Differences: Most of the ingredients called for in the recipes in this book are available in English-speaking countries. However, some are known by different names. Here are some common U.S. American ingredients and their possible counterparts:

✳ Sugar is granulated or castor sugar.

✳ Powdered sugar is icing sugar.

✳ All-purpose flour is plain household flour or white flour. When self-rising flour is used in place of all-purpose flour in a recipe that calls for leavening, omit the leavening agent (baking soda or baking powder) and salt.

✳ Light-color corn syrup is golden syrup.

✳ Cornstarch is cornflour.

✳ Baking soda is bicarbonate of soda.

✳ Vanilla is vanilla essence.

✳ Green, red, or yellow sweet peppers are capsicums.

✳ Golden raisins are sultanas.

Volume and Weight: U.S. Americans traditionally use cup measures for liquid and solid ingredients. The chart, right, shows the approximate imperial and metric equivalents. If you are accustomed to weighing solid ingredients, the following approximate equivalents will help.

✳ 1 cup butter, castor sugar, or rice = 8 ounces = about 230 grams

✳ 1 cup flour = 4 ounces = about 115 grams

✳ 1 cup icing sugar = 5 ounces = about 140 grams

Spoon measures are used for smaller amounts of ingredients. Although tablespoon size varies slightly in different countries, for practical purposes and for recipes in this book, a straight substitution is all that is necessary. Measurements made using cups or spoons always should be level unless stated otherwise.

EQUIVALENTS: U.S. = AUSTRALIA/U.K.

$1/5$ teaspoon = 1 ml	$1/2$ cup = 120 ml
$1/4$ teaspoon = 1.25 ml	$2/3$ cup = 160 ml
$1/2$ teaspoon = 2.5 ml	$3/4$ cup = 180 ml
1 teaspoon = 5 ml	1 cup = 240 ml
1 tablespoon = 15 ml	2 cups = 475 ml
1 fluid ounce = 30 ml	1 quart = 1 liter
$1/4$ cup = 60 ml	$1/2$ inch = 1.25 cm
$1/3$ cup = 80 ml	1 inch = 2.5 cm

BAKING PAN SIZES

U.S.	METRIC
8x1$1/2$-inch round baking pan =	20x4-cm cake tin
9x1$1/2$-inch round baking pan =	23x4-cm cake tin
11x7x1$1/2$-inch baking pan =	28x18x4-cm baking tin
13x9x2-inch baking pan =	32x23x5-cm baking tin
2-quart rectangular baking dish =	28x18x4-cm baking tin
15x10x1-inch baking pan =	38x25.5x2.5-cm baking tin (Swiss roll tin)
9-inch pie plate =	22x4- or 23x4-cm pie plate
7- or 8-inch springform pan =	18- or 20-cm springform or loose-bottom cake tin
9x5x3-inch loaf pan =	23x13x8-cm or 2-pound narrow loaf tin or pâté tin
1$1/2$-quart casserole =	1.5-liter casserole

OVEN TEMPERATURE EQUIVALENTS

FAHRENHEIT SETTING	CELSIUS SETTING*	GAS SETTING
300°F	= 150°C	= Gas mark 2 (very low)
325°F	= 170°C	= Gas mark 3 (low)
350°F	= 180°C	= Gas mark 4 (moderate)
375°F	= 190°C	= Gas mark 5 (moderately hot)
400°F	= 200°C	= Gas mark 6 (hot)
425°F	= 220°C	= Gas mark 7 (hot)
450°F	= 230°C	= Gas mark 8 (very hot)
475°F	= 240°C	= Gas mark 9 (very hot)
Broil		= Grill

*Electric and gas ovens may be calibrated using Celsius. However, for an electric oven, increase the Celsius setting 10 to 20 degrees when cooking above 160°C. For convection or forced-air ovens (gas or electric), lower the temperature setting 10°C when cooking at all heat levels.

rush!
free-year request

BUSINESS REPLY MAIL
FIRST-CLASS MAIL PERMIT NO. 120 BOONE, IA

POSTAGE WILL BE PAID BY ADDRESSEE

Better Homes and Gardens®
Hometown
Cooking™

MAGAZINE
PO BOX 37456
BOONE IA 50037-2456

---

rush!
free-year request

BUSINESS REPLY MAIL
FIRST-CLASS MAIL PERMIT NO. 120 BOONE, IA

POSTAGE WILL BE PAID BY ADDRESSEE

Better
Homes
and Gardens ®

MAGAZINE
PO BOX 37428
BOONE IA 50037-2428